PRAISE FOR
The House That Made Me

"Jarrett has compiled a powerful and must-read collection of meditations on the meaning of home. Each essay in this diverse collection—with writings from rural America to war-torn Sri Lanka—transports the reader on a fresh and riveting journey into the hauntings and heartbreak of childhood. As a whole these varied voices come together in a kind of symphony, a harmonious reminder that individual stories illuminate the connection we all have to one another. Ultimately, these voices together transform this book into its own kind of shelter."

—Jennifer Percy, author of *Demon Camp*,
a *New York Times* Notable Book

"*The House That Made Me* is a revelatory investigation of home, that most beloved and fraught word—how home wields the power to shape us, undo us, remake us. How we carry it, how we let it go. The table of contents for *The House That Made Me* includes some of the finest writers working today, and the worlds that exist inside this tremendous anthology suggest contemporary literature has never been so vital."

—Laura van den Berg, author of *Find Me*

GRANT JARRETT

On Ways of Leaving

"Ruthlessly brilliant writing brings grace to a story smoldering in pain."

—*Kirkus Reviews*

"... an outstanding and devastating new novel ..."

—*Independent Publisher*

ALICE EVE COHEN

On The Year My Mother Came Back

"I love, love, love this book. It's so rich, so real and so moving ... astonishingly wonderful—I was enthralled ... You're a brilliant writer."

—Caroline Leavitt, book critic for *Boston Globe* and *People*, and *New York Times* best-selling author of *Pictures of You*

"A wry, magical memoir about the transcendent power of mother-daughter love."

—*Elle* magazine

"Fiercely brave and unflinchingly honest."

—The Brooklyn Rail

"A perfect book. I want to tell every body, every mother, every daughter, to read it."

—Abigail Thomas, best-selling author of *A Three Dog Life*

KRIS RADISH

"Radish's prose is a joy—energetic, attitudinal, often hilarious and perfectly suited to the anecdotal form."

—Kirkus

"Kris Radish creates characters that seek and the celebrate the discovery of...women's innate power."

—*The Denver Post*

"Radish unrolls a rollicking yet reflective read that adds to her robust repertoire of beloved fiction...What's a reader to do but relish the ride?"

—BookPage

LEE UPTON

On *The Tao of Humiliation: Stories,* named one of the "best books of 2014" by Kirkus Reviews:

"Masterful stories by a writer of great lyrical gifts. Upton focuses on personal relationships, especially the immediacy and estrangement that emerge from the intensity of family life ... Upton specializes in ending her stories with epiphanies that can be searing in their poignancy. These 17 tales explore personal and familial relationships with both pathos and humor—and all are well worth reading."

—*Kirkus* Starred Review

"Poet, essayist, and fiction writer Upton's stories are playful, full of clever allusions that are deftly presented ... Upton's story openings tend to be vivid; they're great hooks ... This is a smart and highly entertaining book."

—*Publishers Weekly* Starred Review

PAMELA ERENS

"Everyone who has the good fortune to pick up one of Erens' (two) novels becomes a fan. Whether writing about teenagers at boarding school (*The Virgins*) or a loner at the end of his tether (*The Understory*), Erens has a gift for making you want to spend time in her characters' company. Then you want to scout her other fans to discuss your good fortune of discovering her talents."

— *Reader's Digest* "23 Contemporary Writers You Should Have Read By Now" (2014)

ROY KESEY

"(A)n exhilarating ramble . . . Kesey's inventiveness is a treat."

—Malcolm Forbes, *The Times Literary Supplement* (London)

"Kesey excels at evoking the geography of the country."

—Jonathan Barnes, *Literary Review* (London)

"Make no mistake: Kesey is a remarkable and serious writer. Stylistically, he sometimes approaches the same category as Don DeLillo or Cormac McCarthy; he is very clearly a poet, and conspicuously original."

—Tod Wodicka, *The National* (UAE)

"A near-direct descendant of Samuel Beckett."

—Jonathan Messinger, *Time Out Chicago*

RU FREEMAN

On *On Sal Mal Lane*, the second, *Extraordinary Rendition: (American) Writers on Palestine.*

"Freeman never strays far from the neighborhood's youngest inhabitants. They are wondrous to behold, with their intelligence, imagination and innocence. I don't know that I've seen children more opulently depicted in fiction since Dickens."

—Christina Garcia for the *New York Times Book Review*

"Ru Freeman has made a book unlike anything I've ever read. It's a great contribution to not only to the conversation about Palestine, but to the larger one about peace and justice."

—Cheryl Strayed, author of *Wild*

TIM JOHNSTON

"Outstanding . . . The days when you had to choose between a great story and a great piece of writing? Gone."

—*Esquire*

"The story [*Descent*] unfolds brilliantly, always surprisingly . . .The magic of his prose equals the horror of Johnston's story; each somehow enhances the other . . . Read this astonishing novel."

—*The Washington Post*

———

the

house

that

made

me

———

the
WRITERS REFLECT
house
ON THE PLACES
that
AND PEOPLE THAT
made
DEFINED THEM
me

Edited by GRANT JARRETT

Published by SparkPress, a BookSparks imprint,
A division of SparkPoint Studio, LLC
Tempe, Arizona, USA, 85281
www.gosparkpress.com

Published 2016
Printed in the United States of America
ISBN: 978-1-940716-31-2 (pbk)
ISBN: 978-1-940716-32-9 (e-bk)

Library of Congress Control Number: 2015956245

Cover design © Julie Metz, Ltd. / metzdesign.com
Cover photo © Ben Thomas / benthomas.net.au
Formatting by Stacey Aaronson / thebookdoctorisin.com

CONTENTS

introduction

Though the definition of the word "home" may be fixed, its connotations are as varied and personal as fingerprints. Even for a particular individual on a given day, its meaning is layered, the lens through which it's viewed in constant motion. And yet there are few things as potent, as visceral and multifaceted as the word and what it represents. Nothing is more highly charged than that first home, the rooms where our memories were born, the place where those first battles were fought and won or lost, where family was defined and redefined, where dreams were born and realized or reluctantly discarded. Rich with our earliest experience, it may have been, may still be, a source of great happiness and great pain, its rooms overflowing with laughter, joy, fear, sorrow. Most likely the image of that first home evokes a hodgepodge of thoughts, sensation and emotions, but regardless, it seems to reach out to us, to draw us ever back. That was certainly my experience when I found myself sitting at my computer some eighteen months ago examining pixelated images of the house where my life began.

Perhaps, in looking back, we hope to gain a new understanding, to rekindle some cherished feeling, to reclaim something lost or discarded. Perhaps we are searching for a way to mend ancient wounds or alleviate some lingering ache for ourselves or for others. Perhaps we yearn to relive a moment of great happiness or recapture some essential part of ourselves: innocence, joy, youth, purity, or at least the fleeting *illusion* of purity that childhood so often constructs.

I didn't know, when I sat at my desk that day and, with nothing but my curiosity to drive me, typed my first address into Google Earth, what I was getting into. I didn't plan to get so caught up in the house and the neighborhood where I was born, I didn't intend to write an essay, and I certainly couldn't have foreseen the book you are now holding. It was the idea of that first home that drew me in, the memories that held me. But if at the onset this was about me, about my past, my home, and my vision, it has long since developed a will and a direction of its own. Thanks to the wonderful authors who have joined me on this journey, taking their own virtual excursions on Google Earth, my private impulse has become something far broader and more universal.

In fact it is the melding of the personal with the universal that makes this collection compelling. And though there are obstacles, setbacks, and tribulations in every life, these are stories of enlightenment and survival. Meg Tuite's raucous neighborhood is a place from which to escape, her oppressive home a motivation to do better. When Pamela Erens recalls her privileged childhood in Chicago, she sees economic and racial divisions, aware, as she looks back, that what we see and feel is colored by our vantage point, that reality is fluid and always subject to interpretation. Tim Johnston's deeply affecting story is a chronicle of regret, but also of understanding and acceptance. And it serves as a reminder that although our histories remain with us, it is, to some degree, up to us to determine how they impact our lives. Ru Freeman takes us to Sri Lanka, drawing us in with her rich sensory descriptions. Along with the heat and discomfort, we can feel the fear, confusion, and grief that permeate her young life. In a country where earthquakes, death threats, and armed soldiers are commonplace, she learns forgiveness. Surrounded by violence, pain, deprivation, and loss, she gains the strength to fashion a future of her own.

But although I might enjoy the challenge, dissecting and describing each of these essays, trying to put into words what makes each one work, would be like writing a melody to describe a symphony. So I think I'll bow out now and let the orchestra begin.

mid-michigan, wacousta road

LEE UPTON

I love the landing.

At first we're coming to earth from outer space, the globe growing larger as we near our destination. The rooftops are miniaturized, the tops of trees look foreshortened and puffy, telephone poles recline, a bridge warps. From this height the fields bristle, like fabric, the texture as pilled as a snagged sweater. The image tilts and flattens and I'm on the road outside my first home, the farmhouse in mid-Michigan where I lived for the first eighteen years of my life.

I have arrived close to the grain of the tarmac. Yards ahead should be a wild apple tree with its wormy sour apples. I can't find the tree, but there are the gullies that rushed with torrents of rainwater in the spring, and to the right stretches the meadow just behind where the horse barn used to be. The bare limbs of the trees look flimsy, as if the past has resolved into a sketch. The sky is dented with the cloudy greyness of a rainy afternoon.

It is November 2008 on the ground, and I am viewing my

first home through Google Earth in December 2014. This representation of the past can be manipulated, rotated. And what we see—unlike a photograph or a film or a digital image we've created—can't be erased. It's there, waiting for anyone. Being at my home in this way seems both touching to me and sinister, sinister because no one on the ground could have known that the land was captured at this moment, as place and time are frozen while we can be in motion, drifting over landmarks or wafting as if with a current, like a jellyfish.

The experience is less like being a jellyfish, however, than like being both a ghost and a voyeur. I can't be seen or heard, a body-less spirit drifting out of time. I'm floating just above the road and shifting direction, invading the privacy of the place.

Google Earth—at least as I'm using it in this location—doesn't reward impatience. The resolution of images is spotty. If I move too quickly the view degenerates, stutters, breaks apart into panes of green and grey. Even with patience, the resolution of the images is like memory: at some points things are brighter and more grained, and the roadside gives back what William Carlos Williams called "the twiggy stuff of bushes." Turn in another direction and everything is a murky mirror ball. The landscape breaks apart and I'm spilled out of street view and up into the globe again.

To see if location affects resolution I check my current home address in Pennsylvania and find that the image on Google Earth is remarkably clear. (There's my car—I must have been home.) I return to Wacousta Road in mid-Michigan and the image blurs, although now the effect strikes me as being like the workings of memory, as if memory needs blank spots, even forgetfulness.

The house I grew up in is white and two-storied with black shutters. The house and yard look unsuspecting, innocent. Seeing the house means that wherever I look memories cloud the view. I remember how in the dining room my father organized bills, impaling them on a nail on a block of wood. He held his head in his hands and sat with those impaled bills before him. For years he and my mother feared that we'd lose the house and farm. I remember my bedroom, how it would become so cold in winter that if I brought a glass of water upstairs the water would be partly frozen by morning.

Even before my mother left the house to live with my family, and then with my sister Faye, she was losing her sight. She still somehow tended the gardens. By then the horse barn and the milk house had been torn down. Even earlier, when the county widened the road, the two enormous maples on the front lawn were toppled.

On my computer screen everything about the house seems foreshortened, compressed. After my mother's funeral members of my family drove to the house although it no longer belonged to us. My sister Lana walked across the lawn and I followed her. We looked into the windows and saw a pool table and posters of naked women. The house had been rented out to a group of young guys. Today other people are living in the house.

What surprises me now is how much the landscape surrounding the house calls to me. To the south, if I move out of street view, I can fly over the woods, which are greenish grey with pines and the mysterious small hills near the creek. From Google Earth the grave markers in Sowle Cemetery (how painfully appropriate the name is) look like tacks pressed into soil. These scenes constrict my throat.

I don't feel rooted but dispersed across this landscape. Like many children I had been lonely. Not a grounded person but a girl who believed things were made of spirits. I invented little rituals and was seldom without a book unless I was in the woods or wading in the creek. What I'm especially grateful for: I had the great good fortune to be left most often to my own devices.

The past—it's like walking into a cobweb. The stickiness of it.

Some of the settings in my fiction draw from what I can see or from what memory helps me see here: the bridge under which I caught minnows in mason jars, the narrow trails in the woods, and the stream where I sat on a boulder for long hours and made secret promises to myself. The landscape is an endless place, yet vulnerable as all landscapes are.

I don't know if I should make too many claims for Googling home. I keep being reminded that the technology is subject to distortion, to what's called "poor resolution," a term that makes me think of how much of the past cannot be resolved. When I use Google Earth to follow the path of the creek below what had been my home or to cross above the fields to the north I think of the stories of farm accidents, of the woman who was said to have poured scalding water over her husband while he slept, of the girl who walked along the road and was struck with a bicycle chain whipped at her by laughing boys in a speeding car. Memory at first seems frail, contorted, and like parts of the landscape here, memory appears grey, with a greenish tinge. Memory sprouts, branches, could go on nearly endlessly, unfolding.

Technology cannot capture the full physicality of this

landscape, but the failures of the technology, its blurring, bending images, create an experience that is resonant and weirdly similar to the workings of memory for me. It's as if time thaws here because so much of what's seen is an inducement to memory, and memory craves motion.

I have recurring dreams. In a variant of those dreams I am inside a house as one wall then another blows down until all the walls are flat around me and I am standing there, unprotected. At first in the dream I'm anxious, but then I see where I am—in the meadow across from the house where I grew up. The meadow grass is high and mist rises from the ground, and everything is a little smudged, and I become calm. Maybe I can think of the dream as telling me what I've been telling myself as I write this: that it was the soil and the air and the water of my first home that claimed me. Even when I want to be dispassionate, when seeing the landscape I react physically before full thoughts form. I can't be dispassionate.

A place, if we've lived there long enough, becomes partly made of memory and can't be reduced to metaphor. It is not a grave or a cradle. I knew as much before I tried Google Earth, but it was good to go home again in such a peculiar way, if only because I saw how memories are incited in this other dimension. I've been thinking about forgetfulness too—how every memory arrives cross-stitched with forgetting, and how forgetting is powerful, as if forgetting is one capacity we can actually master.

I've come back a few more times to Google Earth to see where I grew up. My favorite path: following the creek below our house, a creek where I wandered as a child. Even hovering high above where I walked, I can feel again the wonder of being in that place, the awe of it, the innocence of it, and how all places need protection—and how the world I wanted was there, and will be there, without me.

surviving

wayne avenue

TIM JOHNSTON

3002 Wayne Avenue.

This isn't the house I was born in, or even the house of my earliest memories. My parents were poor graduate students—my mother in the liberal arts, my father in jurisprudence—and they moved around from rented place to rented place and I would not call any of those places we lived in "home" until, finally, just out of law school and ready to begin his practice, my father bought this house on the corner of Wayne Avenue and Dover Street in Iowa City, Iowa.

One spring day he took us to see it. A modest, functionally shaped, newly erected house, 3002 was one of just a few in the newest of neighborhoods on the extreme eastern edge of town, and as we four kids—two older brothers, myself, a younger sister—spilled from the family wagon, there was no happy green lawn for us to run through, no tree limbs to swing from, but instead a great deal of mud and tire tracks and bits of construction debris. A pair of wooden sawhorses stood in the driveway very much in the manner, I remember, of resting ponies. To the east and to the south, for as far as we could see, was open Iowa farmland. To the east, nearly on the horizon, an old gray barn sat alone in all that space.

Years later, when I began writing fiction, this is how I described our new home:

> A January wind was in the seams of the back
> door, moaning eerily. The house, the whole
> neighborhood, kept its back to open farmland
> and bore the first, hardest blows of weather. In
> the spring the air was soaked in the smell of
> soil and manure, and at night you heard the
> cows bawl, and the horn of the freight trains
> was to warn them, William said, to stay off the
> tracks or else. ("Irish Girl")

That spring day, the old barn didn't look so far away but later—two, three years later?—when my two older brothers and I set out for it on foot, convinced by the oldest of us that it was time to run away and what better destination than an old gray barn, it turned out to be much, much farther away than it looked—a trick of depth perception: nothing between the edge of our neighborhood and the barn to suggest distance or scale —nothing but Iowa flatness. (Many years later, after all that flatness had been consumed by developers, and the barn itself repurposed into *The Barn*—four modern-rustic condos—my brothers and I helped our mother in; did we remember then the day we tried, and failed, to reach that structure by foot?)

Memory is shaky—I was four or five—but I believe my mother looked upon the barren lawn of mud, and on the muddied and un-tree-lined street that did not turn nor cul-de-sac but merely ended, as if in exhaustion, in a field of last year's weeds, with a brave face my father did not notice or else chose not to notice; after a lifetime of poverty, of growing up on his grandparents' farm, of an unreliable-at-best father of his own, he was a lawyer at age thirty, had four young children and a wife, and he had bought them this house. What a moment it must have been for him!

The old man had been a high school basketball star and he showed us the place over the garage where he would mount the hoop; who would say he couldn't? Some landlord? This was his house. His. Ours. Here, we would do as we pleased.

In that short story I wrote years later, William is the fictionalized version of my oldest brother, and in the story he is an adopted older brother, which helps to explain to the narrator, his little brother, William's increasingly strange behavior as the two boys grow up in that suburban outpost. When the father of the story gets the politics bug and disappears, as ours did, to faraway Des Moines for long stretches of time, William becomes more defiant, delinquent, violent, and often cruel to the boys' mother, who seems helpless to control her eldest.

William doesn't survive Wayne Avenue. And in a way neither did my brother; by the time my parents were divorced a few years later, my brother was well on his way to a lifetime of terrible decisions and destructive behavior that broke our parents' hearts over and over again. For many years my other siblings and I thought he was just an overgrown bully and jerk —and he was. But he was also an addict, a thing none of us could've conceived of when we were young and living on the outer edge of Iowa City, Iowa.

My oldest brother was many other things too, and he had a life none of us would ever know.

Here's what we did know: he was a genius with mechanical things, including engines and computers; over the years he repaired a number of each of these for me without charge. He had old old friends who would remain loyal to him no matter what, unlike some of us, his worn-down family. Later in life when one of his own troubled sons had a son, he began to dote on the boy, his grandson, and we could see how much he loved this boy and how much the boy loved him. It was astonishing.

But not enough. We could never really believe in this side of him.

We could never believe in him.

In the true—or factual—version of 3002 Wayne Avenue, I kept my head down, literally, most of the time. I'd found that I loved nothing more than a blank sheet of paper: the sound of a good pencil making first lines, the smell of pencil shavings and of little pink eraser debris swept away with the side of the hand. I drew and drew. I drew during class and was considered a slow learner—except that I read very well. I read in class, too, but not the books I was supposed to be reading. I read the books my oldest brother read and passed down to the middle brother who passed them down to me. My eldest brother read so much, it's hard now to imagine how he found the time to get into so much trouble.

One day, on one of those exceptional and exciting weekends when our father was home from Des Moines, as we all sat down for dinner, the phone rang. My father answered. He listened for a moment, said a few words, and hung up. In the next instant my oldest brother and I were wrenched physically

—I want to say by our hair, but maybe it was only our shirts—from our chairs and dragged into the living room and flung to the floor.

My father was a big man; still is, though far less intimidating now, in his seventies, and so mild-mannered you would never guess how quickly his face could turn the shade of a bad fever, or how his voice could make your heart leap out of you and run for its life.

Why didn't the middle brother get hauled from the table? Because he had been with his friends, who were good kids, good students, when our older brother had been destroying the property of one of the neighbor kids—one of those plastic Big Wheels that had become the craze.

Had I been with our older brother at the time?

I said earlier that I kept my head down, that I drew and drew. But the fact is I was a boy and I got into my share of trouble, especially when I followed my big brother around, as a little brother will. I like to believe I didn't partake in the destroying of the Big Wheel, but at the very least I was an accessory just by being with him. And by being his brother.

I was not all good, is the truth. But I hadn't gone all bad, either.

The phone call my father got that night wouldn't be the last, and now I understand that his violence was the expression of a man who'd had a violent father himself, who had grown up in hard Midwestern circumstances. But it was also the expression of a man who believed he'd overcome those circumstances—a man who'd put himself through college and, with the help of his young wife, through law school. Here was a self-made lawyer, a newly minted legislator, and a homeowner—and his sons, he knew, had become the bad kids of the neighborhood. The ones other parents told their kids to stay away from. How embarrassed he must've been.

How humiliated.

When I look at 3002 Wayne Ave. now I see the early chapters of a long, hard story about a father and his oldest son that is still being written today: deep, irreconcilable resentments and disappointments and wrongs and raised hands and hatred and love.

Not long ago my oldest brother was in the VA hospital again—third time in one year—having suffered near respiratory failure and possibly a small heart attack; the man has been dogged by health troubles since the first Gulf War (go to the army or go to jail, was the deal at the time—this deal arranged by our middle brother, the lawyer), and of course from the uncountable cigarettes he's smoked since age twelve. The prognosis this time was dire, and I drove my mother to the hospital, and we met my father in the waiting room, and together the three of us made our way to the ICU.

There he lay, gray-faced and be-gowned and looking far older than he was. He tried to joke with my mother but his voice was ruined from the tube the doctor had recently pulled from his throat. My father sat bedside and said very little. He sat with Mom and they watched as my brother gasped and wheezed in his hospital bed. They watched as I slipped ice chips from a spoon into his chapped lips.

Once, he had been just a little boy. Their son, their first-born. My mother had read to him and my father had taught him to ride a bike—perhaps on that safe stretch of Wayne Avenue that died in a field of weeds.

What did they remember, sitting there in that hospital room?

What would they remember if, after all, my brother didn't survive?

155

ANTONYA NELSON

I grew up at 155 N. Roosevelt, Wichita, Kansas. The image online, these days, is very close to the way I remember the house and yard from childhood: huge, a tad untended, sagging here and there (it is more than a hundred years old), in endless need of some upkeep or other.

The way I remember it from childhood, and the way I revisit it in adulthood.

This house is located in the heart of Wichita, within walking distance of downtown, a neighborhood of stately old homes and outdated businesses perpetually teetering between gentrification and demolition, succumbing to both in equal measure: hopeful coffee shop or B&B; trash-strewn parking lot or invasion of slovenly low-rent tenants.

Our house has always been shrouded, lurking inside the greenery of both trees and vines. My father hated grass; every Christmas a new conifer was added to the yard, which was and is a virtual forest. Beneath the upper canopy grow vines and poison ivy. In those dark places hide possums, raccoons, rabbits, and all manner of birds, for whom he built elaborate houses. The only bit of wildlife he abhorred were the average city dwelling types, pigeons—he was forever hanging rubber snakes from the gutters, installing veritable beds of nails beneath the rafters—and squirrels, who kept invading the starling houses.

He built both bat and owl boxes, too, neither of which took.

My mother still lives in that house. My siblings and I still gather there. Over the most recent Christmas, after a few bottles of wine, after our mother was safely tucked away, my siblings and I started talking about our hidden lives in that house. There are five of us, and our ages stretch across nearly two decades; at one point my mother could claim to have one of us in jail, another in diapers. As a result, our memories of our childhoods are quite varied; we were often going through very different stages. Just like the creatures in the yard outside— foxes, most recently added to the list—we'd been capable of existing for long spans of time without being seen.

What I mean is: the house is so huge and maze-like as to defy omniscience. Four full floors, at least two thousand square feet each. One simply cannot know it all. One cannot patrol the place adequately; as soon as you secured the first floor, for example, heading up to the second, well, somebody could sneak from the basement into the elevator shaft and elude you. Say you had made certain no one was on the third floor, up there in the former servants' quarters. As soon as you headed down the back stairs, that person in the elevator shaft could shimmy up and into the attic kitchen. There are so many ports of entry and egress that no single sensibility could feel assured. Anybody could be up to anything.

It was a place either terrible or terrific for playing Hide and Seek, depending on whether or not you were *It*. You might be *It* for a long, long time...

Into the house came the unknown, the runaway friend or illicit lover. Plenty of sanctioned guests came and went, as well: the castoffs and black sheep, needy grad student or indigent relative. They stayed in the attic, in the basement, on the couches (at least ten of those, here and there). The buxom blonde exchange student from Germany, for instance, who, charged with babysitting the younger of us, was supplying drugs to the older. Hannelore: she sent us all to the doctor for hugely painful shots when she contracted hepatitis B. Or the cousins, some of my father's, some of my mother's, adults at turning points—divorce, parole, bankruptcy—in need of temporary asylum.

Besides the five official doors—front, side, portico, back door, other back door—there were sneakier portals: the attic dormer window, which meant a tricky feat of scaling the (rotted) trellis outside our parents' bedroom window. The kitchen window, accessed by standing on the (broken) air conditioner outside and jimmying with a stick. Easiest yet dirtiest was the coal chute, a loud metal lid like a manhole cover on the driveway, a filthy slide into a basement room filled, not with coal in the 1970s, but broken furniture and toys. Sometimes there was a car parked over that route. Sometimes you'd be wearing white...

Along with people we kept pets in that house that went unknown by our parents. We sneaked in mice (stolen from a local pet store, secreted in coat pockets, housed in the furnace room for months without detection, meanwhile multiplying by the dozens); our own cat Ink gave birth to a litter she somehow knew would not survive, and so deposited them around the place for us to find later, little defective kitten corpses, one in the wine cellar, one in the fireplace grate, one behind the bar-room fridge. There are probably a few others still, mere skeletons... Last Christmas, over drinks, the five of us siblings took a tour of our secret places, the nooks and crannies where we stashed drugs and Penthouses and the extra keys.

Keys to the house. To the cars. To the trailer in the drive. Where once a beaten girlfriend of my older brother lived for a few months. Busted only when the extension cord from the pantry was discovered in a spring thaw.

Even now, the house exudes a sense of multiple over-lapping stories; there's always somebody awake there, doing something, whether it's three in the afternoon or three in the morning, fixing a leak, crying in a closet, having a clandestine phone call. Listening illicitly in to that same call. These days, it's because of the 24/7 care of my mother, a whole fleet of women wearing scrubs, who all know the lockbox combination, in addition to the larger extended family, who visit from far and near. The playroom in the basement has been in constant use for fifty years, the grandchildren now roaring around the Matchbox cars, hosting tea parties or donning clattery heels and feather boas, setting up the Fisher-Price little people that were brand new back when. Down there as well, another generation is hustling pool or bashing Ping-Pong balls or spinning the foosball handles; up on the attic roof the next batch of teens sneaks its smokes and drinks. When the doorbell chimes its familiar tune—a few of the chimes clunking deadly, some errant wiring offering up the same bunk melody—a different bunch of dogs starts howling. Around the same kitchen table a group gathers to eat or play cards—bridge, if my mother is still awake; poker, after she's gone to bed—or fill pill boxes or do homework or pay bills or strategize for the next meal.

You could get lost in such a place; small children routinely do, their first visit. You can hear them crying, having wandered into a room or up a flight of stairs, suddenly alone and without direction, navigating what seemed a safe enough journey, hardly any number of steps beyond their parent, and yet... "Mom?!" comes the squall, and three different Moms pop up, ready to aid the search.

I mean, we've all been there ourselves. Unhappily, or happily, lost and unseen in that vast magnificent place.

this brown,
this green

RU FREEMAN

I agree to write an essay because I think that whatever it is that Google Earth can show me cannot compare to the images in my mind. I imagine that the imprecision of a program that captures only what it can discern as physical demarcations will be a poor substitute for the alterations made on topography by a culture such as mine.

I download and I click. I am right: this address, 601/2 Havelock Road, Colombo 06, Sri Lanka, appears only as an anonymous rooftop set into a landscape that is mostly brown. The mud-colored streets sided by dull, taupe homes and shops, a few splotches of withered green to calm the eye, and that is it. No yellow-tinged araliya, no purple bougainvillia, no orange fruited thambili trees, and none of the myriad hues of green that are the first thing you notice about the country as you glide in off the Indian ocean, cross the empty beaches and land on the 270-mile by 150-mile island that holds my home. The landmark that heralds the turn-off to the dead-end street of my childhood, however, is clearly represented with its blue roof and rows of white cars for sale, just as it is in the instructions we now give on-call taxi drivers as they hurtle down the one-way road that accesses this lane down which I once lived, and which now lives on as Sal Mal Lane in my second novel, entitled *Sal Mal Lane*. What the trader demolished in order to sell cars for roadways that can barely carry them—the batik shop run by the bow-legged widow, Mrs. Wettasinghe, the hut she had gifted an old, impoverished couple, Lucas and Alice, these homes and their inhabitants—exists only in that novel.

My home sits at the heart of that book, and I used a novelist's sleight of hand to censor the small and large deprivations, both material and emotional, and to imbue the Herath family with the best of what my own family once shared—the philosophical, music-making oldest son, the boy wordsmith who came after, the only girl who was both boon and bane, the distracted teacher, the mostly absent civil servant, and the open-door policy that brought all manner of misfits into our beds and onto our sparse couches and hard cement floors over the years. I brought to life the people who had passed on down that lane, and gave them stories they had never lived. It was all true and it was all imaginary.

The life that unfolded in reality more closely resembles the hues of the bleak map that I look at now. Our lives were difficult in fundamental ways: food was there or it was not, we did not ask; I went to school often on tea and nothing else and many were the days when my lunch was so unpalatable that I would use a trick of the mind to eat it: this is my last meal, I'd say to myself, my last meal in prison, I'd add, turning what was distasteful into something delicious. In this way I learned to love pumpkin curry and the green-leaved malluns I loathed. In this way I learned to lead lives beyond the one I had in that house, in stations both higher than might have been expected of a skinny, hot-headed, boy-girl, and much lower than were hoped for me by my parents.

Some of those dreams took place up on the roof that marks my house on Google Earth. Climbing the roof was the kind of excitement that was permissible only because my mother had once been a girl who, like me, had been a dark-skinned dare-devil who could outrun the boys, and climb higher than any of them. I'd shimmy up the steep slopes even as my older brothers watched from the flatter surfaces beneath, and from its peak I'd talk about what I could see from such heights. The whereabouts of Aunty Mallika, who lived next door and routinely yelled at us, the exact ripeness of the fruit on the guava trees next door, and the specific strength of the roots of the ivy that separated that guava tree from us, the means I would use to scale it, whether Uncle Gomez (who owned all the homes down the street) was setting off on some errand or not, and what that might mean for all manner of shenanigans we could get up to at the far end of the lane which abutted his house. Mostly, I liked going there alone, a diary in hand, to hide under the one bit of shade that could be found where the asbestos of the new roof reached beneath the red tiles of the old one, or crouch in the overhang of the Sal Mal tree that belonged to the people behind our house.

The roof is barely visible now on the Google map, buried as it is beneath the reach of that very tree, the tree that caused years of discord between its owners and my family. Its branches were heavy and laden with flowers that rained down into the drains and gutters of our home, and its foliage blocked the sun enough to provide a welcome shade, yes, but also made it impossible to dry clothes on the lines that sagged in deep fatigue between the sour biling tree and the posts in our own backyard. Its tangled jack-in-the-beanstalk vines were the stuff of dreams for us children, but it seemed to represent something more ominous than waiting giants for our parents. My mother could be found ordering some hired day-laborer to wrench the gnarled tendrils down, or setting fire to papers infested with termites in great bonfires that singed the greenery above, and my father would rail with the best of them at the bastards who had so little sense of neighborly duty that our distress would not occur to them.

And yet. There was the matter of the ever-forty-year-old, ever-bare-bodied son of those neighbors, the one whom we kids feared, the one who was visible in the half-lit interiors of his house when I climbed up on the wall between our homes, my feet placed just so between the sharp shards of glass embedded into the concrete, and peered in. Their house was more decrepit then than ours now is, and the sooty walls of the kitchen in which he usually hovered were only made worse by the equally filthy cook who cackled and shooed me from within. What they did all day, he, his parents, this cook, I don't know. We called him The Knouer's Son and I worried that he, tall as he was, could see me showering, that he was watching our house, that he had designs on my person or my brothers. He, like his parents' tree, occupied a great space in my life. I don't know, now, where he went, or his family; I only see, when I climb up on the roof, that there is a landscaped garden that laps against a beautiful house. And the only thing that remains of that time is the Sal Mal tree.

I take up that battle on my father's behalf, asking not for the felling of the tree but for the pruning of the branches that hang over our house. I find a man who scales the tree that is covered in stinging large red ants, and cuts them down, and I find common ground with the new owner who agrees to pay for the poor man's labors. My sister-in-law quips that it is must surely be the power of the visiting American that can so easily dissolve all of our previous acrimony. Perhaps, I think, it is only the American way of asking for what one wants in such matters, over the Sri Lankan way of expecting what is right to come to pass that makes the difference. I am grateful for the sunlight that now pours into the backyard, but I mourn the loss of the shade and beauty of this sacred tree, the tree that gave my book its name.

Such contradictions are what my family is made of. On this visit, my father who has done his bit to keep his granddaughters off his leaking, broken, unsafe roof—even as I urge them on—asks for their help to bring down the harvest from his plantain tree which holds the long stem full of combs over the low asbestos covering over the back of the house. I watch four of his many granddaughters, aged eleven to fourteen, wrestle with the long flat leaves, the pliant yet bulky trunk of the banana tree, the milky insides that spurt and stain their shirts. I watch my brother's friend, who had been summoned to fix my father's computer, climb this same roof in his khaki pants, polo shirt, and dress shoes, and join them in the tussle. Nobody complains.

How can an aerial photograph tell us anything of real value?

There were wars waged here, in this house and in this neighborhood. Carols and Buddhist and Hindu prayers were uttered in times of peace in houses that were burned to the ground in a single day that carved a permanent scar on the conscience of a nation. In this house, my mother's raging brother was once tied to his bed at the back of the house during an ugly, hopeless night, the same place where Old Mr. Sylvester, an invalid, was carried in on his bed during the anti-Tamil riots of 1983 that left part of his house in ashes. Here my oldest brother lit incense, dreamed of a career in music, sang bhajans, played U2 chords on his guitar and Mozart on the piano, and never seemed to be touched by the harsh winds of disenchantment that blew through the house. Here also my second older brother flung furniture around and wrote love poetry to a succession of girls, declaring an equal, everlasting devotion to each one of them. The half-wall in the verandah, over which that brother tripped and nearly lost his life, was the same one on which I sat in the light of a full moon, all of seventeen, and experienced a kiss that asked not for the body but for the soul itself.

The space allocated for a garage once housed my father's Citroen, a heap of junk that he prized, and which ran perhaps twice in its lifetime before it was sold, a sale and removal I remember watching as it transformed my father's features, a dream of a sort being hauled up and taken away. That fifteen-by-ten-foot garage was turned into a kitchen and a living room by my American husband and me, a setup that rivaled the functionality of Ikea's small-space designs in a quintessentially Sri Lankan way, with space for a half-blonde baby, for entertaining strangers from Poland to America, *and* a shrine to the Buddha with a lamp lit each night and no fear of fires that could ignite our cane and wood furniture or the paper accoutrements of graduate students. That garage emptied when I left, taking my parents' first grandchild with me, and returned to the decay it had embraced when my father's car had been hauled off. It became my oldest brother's mad sanctuary when he could neither bring himself to divorce his first wife, nor marry the second. Somewhere into one of its corners my mother tucked the wedding albums and framed wedding photographs, the memorabilia of my other brother's first marriage, items she could not bring herself to discard with the same alacrity with which he had released his vows. In that garage, piled high up each wall with simmering piles of papers and books, my brothers sat, one at each end of the room, cigarette smoke thick in the air, while I watched them pass pages of my first novel to each other, reading through the night, one declaring the book was useless, the other asking for permission to finish before commenting. A book I never published.

Around the corner from our street, by the bridge, there was a checkpoint that grew from a hut with a single policeman to a monstrosity that filled with armed soldiers. There were soldiers in the house next door, and informants down the streets, death threats arrived at my parents' home, my brother was jailed, we fled and we returned. From this house my parents heard that their second son was contesting an election in the north where the war was raging, suicide-bombers were being groomed for destruction, and the roadways were jeweled with landmines. In this house my parents heard that their oldest son was missing in the tsunami and, later, that he had survived. Year after year, their children, we, brought them news both devastating and joyful: the end of marriages, the discovery of cancer, accolades around the writing we had all learned to do as a way of surviving the earthquakes of our childhood, the birth of granddaughters. In that house my mother nurtured thousands of students, turning American colleges and universities from Pomona to Princeton into household names.

This was a home where people were as likely to be driven out as they were to be welcomed, often the same people. The mother who gave me every last cent she had was also the same one who smashed her fist against the door between the apartment I'd carved for myself out of her house; a glassless rectangle marks the spot. Yet what it recalls is not so much her hurt at the time, but the fact that it began to serve the function of passing gifts, written messages, telephone calls, and voices through from one side to the other. These were the ways in which we learned that nothing was permanent: the sometimes ostracized, other times included, the threatened and those who found solace, we all served some good at some point. Many things were broken, and yet in our broken state we found ways to be deserving of love, and to love. There were strengths, but in far greater measure there were frailties in this house, in this neighborhood, in the country itself. And though we could never do the same for ourselves, we had no choice but to forgive someone every single day.

I gaze and I gaze at the photograph that Google Earth provides. In it I can find nothing but rudimentary information about a place devoid of meaning. It reminds me of our addiction to access, our insatiable need to collect information rather than knowledge, our preference for the quickly summoned explanation—who cares who provides it, or with what intent—over an immersion in a place. This is how we read the news from other places, this is how we skim the world, thinking that all there is to know can be known from our desks, couches, tables. We believe that if we tap into a fad (neem for the face, yoga for our spirits, etc.), we have experienced a culture. We click like on a Facebook photograph and think we know a place. We imagine that following a Twitter feed makes us understand both personal and national revolutions and the bitter sorrow of a failed aftermath.

But Google Earth cannot show you the split slat underneath the insufficient cushions on the hard couches my mother bought with her few funds. It cannot tell you that she strove to match the vomit green of those cushions to the cream and green curtains unevenly hemmed with the help of her aging eyes. It cannot tell you that I take those cushions and use them to extend the breadth of the double bed that my father had built for my six-foot husband when we were first married, so that it can accommodate the tangle of the butterscotch bodies of my three daughters and their mother as we sleep at night under a mosquito net in the one room with a functioning fan. It cannot tell you that for a girl like me, who grew up with only the cool cement floor as relief from Colombo's interminable heat, this arrangement is a luxury. It cannot tell you that each night before I fall asleep, I imagine my mother's joy at this innovation, at the sheer usefulness of her cushions. It cannot tell you that she lived and died believing that the elegant and beautiful life she had imagined for herself, in a home that did not resemble this one, would one day be hers. It cannot tell you that I was witness to the things that haunted her, and the things that undid her, and that I understand her grief in a time when she is not here for me to tell of that awakening.

Google Earth shows you a dark roof in a crowded brown landscape. We do not live there.

battling fear
and gravity

GRANT JARRETT

I was zipping around the planet on Google Earth one afternoon when I decided to pay a virtual visit to the home that inhabits my earliest recollections. A sturdy brick row house on the corner of two tree-lined streets in Pennsylvania's Lehigh Valley, it didn't look nearly as shabby as I'd feared, even after so many years. The first thing I recalled as I navigated that still faintly familiar block was the day I decided to take the training wheels off my bicycle and learn to ride. At the age of five, alone with my hand-me-down two-wheeler, I went out to the sidewalk next to the house, stepped over the bike's frame, and with a persistence I didn't know I possessed—pedal, fall, pedal, fall, etc.—struggled with my balance until I was able to remain upright and, to a limited degree, in control.

But as I sat at my desk blurrily visualizing my younger self and reliving that minor early victory, other memories began to creep forward from whatever dark, distant corner they usually occupy. That was the house where, after a long, noisy quarrel with my mother, my father locked himself in the attic. He remained up there for hours, maybe longer, refusing to come down or allow anyone else up, ignoring the pleas of his wife and children. When my mother called through the door to ask if she could bring him some dinner, he responded with silence. A few months later, perhaps it was longer, I lay on the living room couch suffering with measles, sweating, shivering, weak, dizzy, my vision failing, or seeming to, watching as my hazy, inverted father stomped out, suitcase in tow, without a word or a glance in my direction. I'd just turned six and didn't understand what was happening. He was leaving us for the last time.

Before the divorce was final or custody decided, my mother and father had another fight, which ultimately advanced through the small alcove just off the kitchen—the alcove where my father had whipped us with his belt when we'd committed what he considered a particularly serious offense—out our back door, and onto the sidewalk. A couple minutes later my brothers and I heard some muffled shouting. When my mother limped back inside her leg was bleeding, her stockings were torn, and the heel had broken off one of her shoes. In an effort to avenge her injuries, to vent their own anger, or both, my two eldest brothers went out to my father's car with their pocket-knives and shredded his seats and dashboard.

As I zoomed in on the home's white wooden front door, I recalled the day my father came from wherever he now lived to take his five sons out for some ice cream, and how my father stood silently watching while my mother lined us up, looked us in the eyes, and asked us, one at a time, "Do *you* want to go with your father?" What choice did we have but to say, with our father looking on, that we didn't want to go? And then I remembered another day, some time after that, when my mother wasn't home but for some reason I was and my father stopped in again, this time to ask me to go to lunch with him. My grandmother, my mother's mother, who lived with us throughout my childhood, told him he couldn't take me. He pleaded and argued and somehow got me to go outside with him, but she refused to let me go. On the little walkway leading to the sidewalk in front of our house, my tiny grandmother gripping one arm and my father tugging on the other, these two adults pulled me back and forth like two children fighting over a doll or playing tug of war. I was probably seven years old by that time and I'm sure I was confused, and I was probably afraid, though of what I'm not quite so sure, perhaps just another crack in the rickety structure of my life.

That was the bedroom where the nightmares began. The house burnt down again and again. Sometimes I'd call out for my mother or go downstairs to get her. Sometimes, I'd lie and tell her I'd had the dream when I hadn't, when I couldn't find a way to ask directly for whatever it was I wanted.

Then there was the frigid day the following winter when one of my brothers, Eric, I believe, saw our cat creep under the hood of a neighbor's car and disappear. When the neighbor emerged from his house and started walking toward the car my two oldest brothers frantically warned him that our cat was in there, under his hood, or somewhere underneath, where things twisted and turned, maybe trying to stay warm. This man we really didn't know assured us, with perhaps a hint of condescension—we were just stupid kids, after all—that what we were suggesting simply wasn't possible. I can see him now, standing next to his car in his gray overcoat and hat, shaking his head as he opened his car door, got in, and turned the key. His engine's fan sliced our beloved cat into a bloody purée.

As I studied the home's pillared front porch I remembered how we would sit out there and watch the rain and the lightning and listen to the thunder. Sometimes, after the worst of the storm had passed and only a gentle drizzle remained, my brother Scott and I would drop Popsicle sticks in the gutters and follow them until the water washed them down a drain, or until we just lost interest. Then I remembered the time our next-door neighbor, Mr. Pendry, enraged by my oldest brother's afternoon piano playing, forced his way into our house, pulled Keith off the piano bench and put him in a half nelson, the veins in Mr. Pendry's neck bulging like flooded streams. He held my brother there, shaking and cursing and as nearly out of control as anyone I'd seen, with the possible exception of my own parents. One afternoon months later, that same neighbor's daughter was sitting on the curb holding her baby brother on her lap and absently playing with him. When a car came roaring down the street she jumped up. Timmy fell off her lap and onto the pavement. The car's tires squealed and my brother Scott and I screamed for someone to come help as the boy's sister ran away. Or did she just stand there, in shock or simply bored, while her brother wailed, blood cascading from his head? Not all memories are clear or consistent. Probably none are entirely reliable. I do know that some months later I shot Timmy, who'd recovered from his injuries, in the mouth with my potato spud gun. He ran home crying and I got in trouble.

A brief exploration of the home's separate garage with its shingled roof and tarnished rain gutters exhumed the memory of the weeks when an Archway deliveryman parked his truck there. The garage door barely closed with his truck in it and my mother had to park her car out on the street. I remembered wondering what was going on between my mother and this stranger, and why he couldn't park his truck somewhere else (didn't he have a house and a garage of his own?), though I did enjoy the sugar cookies he sometimes brought us. I can still picture the package they came in, the cellophane wrapping, the label with bold white letters on a red background.

What I didn't recall as I studied that old house is feeling helpless or hopeless, though I think it makes sense that I would have. It may just be a trick of memory. Still, I suppose everyone's been exposed to some unpleasantness. And hasn't every child known sadness and disappointment? Hasn't every child experienced loss? I may not have known it then, but the world is rife with suffering far more profound than my own. Still, I find myself struggling to define the practical value of that knowledge.

A year or so after we moved out, to another house in another town, the living room ceiling of our home on Highland Street collapsed, or so I was told. My father has been dead for several years now and I don't believe my mother ever forgave him. My brothers and I have little to say to one another and two months ago, at the age of ninety-three, my mother passed away. I was sitting with her, holding her hand when her weary body finally shut down. In some ways I guess I'm still battling fear and gravity, though I'm not sure I'm as buoyant or as brave now as I was at five. But the house is still there, looking much the same as the one I recall.

waxing din rises
from the asphalt

MEG TUITE

Farwell Avenue is a long stretch of clapboard and stucco houses in beige, yellow, beige, light blue, beige, and white with trim in gun-stained grays and revolver black, backing into shadows of elm trees and lilac bushes settling up against wood to show how perfect the crew-cut emerald coiffed lawns buffer sounds of family in summer.

Behind glass and wood, kids are beaten, parents stare into universal holes of what might have been, suicide, a load of laundry they forgot in the dryer, or if there's enough bologna and bread for next day's lunch. Mom irons shirts, wonders how many years she's been married. Dad walks around nude, wonders if he's gained weight, finds a mirror after each meal.

Our older brother, Carl, names the backyard 'Farwell Arms'. He paints a version of the Chicago Cub's bleachers with fans, row after row of two-inch people in oranges, blues, yellows, and pinks with mouths open, holding banners and hotdogs on the side of the garage door. He sets up a baseball diamond in the yard with throw pillows as bases and chalk marks the pitcher

37

mound. Two Johns and a James come over and play baseball while my sister, Lisa, and I practice roller-skating backward. We listen to these altar boys scream, spit and swear. James' face turns valentine's red, his voice raises three opera octaves and shrieks, 'JESUS,' whenever he gets a strike. We laugh and get in the way with overt defiance until Lisa gets a hardline baseball to the knee, spews back 'goddamnit' and 'cockface' that makes James' face purple and the boys' attempts at cursing sound like creaking doors or knocking radiators. Mom stumbles out, bats heads and Dad carries Lisa to the car, the hospital, the welcome swirl of emergency hurls through thin air, makes tomorrow an easier coffin to settle thoughts in. Lisa's leg cast becomes the framework rather than the lucid force of another cloudless sky demanding lists to be compiled, beds made, toilets scrubbed, the sapping endless debris of certainty that nothing new will transpire.

Mom pays Lisa and Carl a dollar a day in summer to clean out the garage. Bags of cement, paint cans, rusted saws, clothes, newspapers, artifacts busy with the moan of flies, sweat the stench of unclenched centuries. Soot and swirling hands unhinge this vault as Lisa and Carl fondle and examine objects before dumping them into garbage bins. Lisa finds a salvaged beauty under a pile of bricks. She and Carl huddle together, faces animated, spit, laugh, open and close pages whenever anyone gets close. 'Go to hell,' they hiss at me when I want in on the deal. Within a few hours the word is out and kids stream down the alley toward the garage. Lisa procures a quarter and lets one body in at a time as Carl holds the coveted magazine and turns pages. One of the Russell boys snatches it and starts running. Carl never fights, soft as a cushion. He goes down.

Not Lisa. She trips Tim Russell and rips it out of his hands. They count their money later and split four bucks. Carl locks the magazine up in his safe with the cash. I've known the code since Lisa broke it to steal his Indian nickel collection for candy. Carl is a genius, but not at codes. His birthday cracks it open.

I am entranced. I take the magazine to my room and close the door. The mutilated magazine is in a foreign language, but black and white visuals cradle me. Hairless, sausage-shaped man lies on bed. He picks up phone. Pretty woman in maid's outfit with a priest's cardboard white neckpiece pinned to her long hair wearing a skirt shorter than my nose, and high, high heels knocks on door. Sausage man opens door. He beckons her in. She has a duster in hand. He lies on the bed while she leans over and dusts a lamp with no underwear on. Her butt exposed has me feeling something moving from nether regions. Sausage man gets up and sausage fingers unzip the maid's costume. She turns with hand over the big O of her mouth. Sausage man does things to her that I follow step by step. Maid is doing things to the sausage on sausage man that I'm not sure wouldn't do some damage. Seas are rising from my fingers. Pee is not the only thing that comes from this location. I replay the script until I'm rocking like Nelson Klasky who flailed around one day on the floor like a fish in a boat. Teacher said it was epilepsy. I wonder what it would be like to have epilepsy all the time.

Farwell Avenue is filled with kids. Some houses are louder than others. Some houses house whole families with six to ten raucous kids that are quieter in spring and summer because they are kicked out until dinnertime. Most kids go to the

Catholic school a mile from the house. Offspring are stumbling obstacles that wrestle around Lunt Park, a few blocks away. The same damn clouds bristle and puff all summer. Faces are blustery and overfed. They crouch inside themselves. Tangled teeth, twisted grins, and panic are hooded under thundering, moronic curses as cans of beer and cigarettes are sucked on.

In one house a boy stutters backhand after backhand until he becomes still as the pillars framing the exterior of his house. He goes to school with swollen eyes. He doesn't move his arms when he walks. Two of his teeth are missing. His mom's a nurse, but never takes him to the dentist. His dad picks up the newspaper in his robe and pajamas each morning. The boy walks to school. Everyone walks to school. I leave the same time as him most days. I slacken my pace so he won't have to talk to me. It won't be good for either of us.

In one house a girl's bony face is all eyelids and blush with stuffed animals planked against a canopied headboard, dolls leering from shelves around her pink on pink room, dolls sitting at tiny tables with teacups, dolls in rockers, dolls in doll beds who inhabit a miniature house, four stories high, all covered in bandages and blankets. 'They're cold, so cold,' the girl says. 'This is the cancer ward. Don't sneeze.' She tells Lisa and me that she gets a new doll every time she's in the hospital. Lisa says, 'You must live in the hospital. This is a Chinese plastic factory's nightmare.' The girl's face, elongated and sharp, squints her watery, brown eyes and smirks at Lisa. "I have more dolls than you'll ever see in your entire ugly life. You're just a trashbag is what you are and your mom's crazy. Your bangs are crooked and your clothes are pioneer crap that no store would ever sell." Lisa starts to bulk up, hands become fists as she moves toward the skeletal girl. I grab Lisa before she jumps her. "You're a funeral waiting to happen," says Lisa just as the girl's mom comes in with cookies. We run past her and don't look back. I slow down and study the sloppy tragedy of my sister in front of me. We are choppy, hand-me-down girls. Mom sometimes shuts her bedroom door and doesn't open it for days. I wanted to hold at least one of the dolls and brush its hair.

Keep moving down the block. One kid is so white that he makes white look psychedelic. His dad keeps Christmas lights up all year because they are lazy. This family is quiet, hazy, like one of those silent movies. A girl lives in the house that only Carl has seen. Why doesn't she go to school? asks Lisa. Does she have that disease where she randomly swears in church or at people in malls? I ask. Lisa wants to know what color her hair is and if she is fat? The vague family waits for snow so their dad can hit the switch and illuminate the outline of their tired home from December 1st to January 2nd. Then it goes black again, disappears. A fog lifts for one month to reveal an island outlined in flashing blue, red, green, yellow, like snorkeling.

Two adults, called couple, are soused by Great Dane accumulation. They don't have kids. They are show people who show dogs, not people. They sell puppies for fountains of money. Lisa stalks and wearies them with love. We don't have cash so Lisa babysits nine puppies who slobber and pile over each other like a stack of wriggling fish. She wraps herself around one of these long-limbed wrinkled creatures, calls her Elsa, and Dad either says NO or no. Lisa is loud and torments everyone when angry. Elsa is an avalanche just like her. The dog eats shoes, garbage and corners of couches. Her tail is a weapon, but has to be bandaged once after she knocks down an armoire filled with trophies. She rummages around the house until she is no more disruptive or invisible than the rest of us.

I sometimes hide in the garage and read while everyone is out. The words on each page blast me further and further from this house, neighborhood, country, planet. I move from corner to corner with the sunlight until shadows puddle over words, the screen door slams and Mom yells for me and siblings to get home. Six o'clock. Time for dinner. I close my book, fold a corner over and stuff it into my shorts.

And always, always, before I get up and go inside to wash my hands, I press my skinned knees tight to my chest, rock back and forth, and imagine what route I will take when I am old enough to escape this block.

belonging to a place, once lost

PATRICIA JABBEH WESLEY

I always wanted my own home, something that belonged to
me and my children, to me and the man I would marry.
Perhaps this is because I grew up a stepchild in my father's
house. In Liberia, the life of a stepchild was difficult. Step-
mothers or stepfathers seemed incapable of shielding other
people's children coming to them through marriage from abuse.
And fathers or mothers who assigned us these unwilling parents
did nothing to protect us. I used to wonder if that had to do
with the inability of the Liberian government to enforce laws
protecting children. So, for me, a real home was something I
would have to build. I wanted a place where I could help my
children belong, where they could feel the warmth I never
knew as a child, a home where the doors always remained
opened for them no matter what.

So, in 1987, my husband Mlen-Too and I began building our
first home in a place called Pagos Island, a neighborhood in one
of Monrovia's suburbs of Congo Town. We had gone through

seven years of marriage, three rental homes, and an apartment during grad school in the US. This new home would be our first real home, built for us. In our time, Pagos Island was a small island of rolling hills that boasted its share of affluent people in Monrovia. But the island was more important in the 1970s when, before the 1980 military coup, the daughter of Liberia's nineteenth president lived on Pagos Island. Her former home was now occupied by squatters and caretakers as we, the new generation, made this island community our home.

I loved a place that was part of the larger Monrovia, but separated in a way by its interesting terrain. The island is partially surrounded by the Mesurado River, which meanders around Monrovia and its charming metropolis. Even though the Mesurado is not the largest river near Monrovia, it is the most overwhelming landmark of the city, almost omnipresent. In many parts of the city, it could be just a strip of water, and at other points, a wide, swift river. At the back of our new home, the river was a huge dark flowing body of water, rushing at times and, at other times, still. But it was filled with crocodiles, blue crabs, and fish. It was not uncommon to spot a crocodile hiding in the swamps of the red mangrove Rhizophora mangle trees behind our home. On a good sunny day, I would walk to the river's banks during low tide and watch the fish do their flips as if in competition. I could never tell why, but it could be the heat of the river that made them do these robotic flips. I have always been a lover of the country and of bushes wherever I lived. It was therefore refreshing to look out the living room window in the evenings and see the vast swampland and the river.

But at the front of the island, the river was a mass of

swampland connecting the island to the main Congo Town. There was a small pipe bridge that gave residents access to the main Tubman Boulevard and to greater Congo Town. There was one drawback to our lovely secluded neighborhood, however. With just one small gravel road for driving or walking, we were locked in, something we became more aware of in the early days of Charles Taylor's bloody attack on Monrovia during the Liberian civil war.

We built our home in this secluded, peaceful place just three years after our return home from graduate school. Those were difficult times in Liberia. Samuel K. Doe, Liberia's military leader, was still in the process of reinventing himself from a violent military leader into a civilian President after the controversial 1985 elections. Instead of stepping down as military leader, he allegedly rigged the elections, and became a civilian president. But even as a civilian president, he continued like the violent military dictator that most leaders of military coups become, killing his enemies, locking up others he could not kill, and keeping the nation the violent military state that Liberia had become. My husband and I returned home to this uncertainty. But we were determined to build our own home from the dregs of our meager salaries.

Our three quarters of an acre on Pagos Island was at the border between the Mesurado River and Paynesville City. A once forgotten piece of land, this was the perfect place to call home. In January, 1988, just one year before the onset of the Liberian civil war, we moved our two young children—Besie, then four years old, and Mlen-Too II, three—into the three-bedroom, two-bath home. Due to the hard times and not wanting to continue paying rent, we moved into the home before it was fully completed. Our third child, a son, Gee, would be born a year later.

We were young professors at the University of Liberia with hopes of returning to the US for more education, but for now, this was home. One of the first things I did after we moved in was to plant trees—fruit trees, not just shade trees as is done in other countries. During the early months of 1988, I would purchase trees for the yard during my weekly food shopping to the Red Light Market grounds in Paynesville every weekend. Paynesville was the larger suburb a few miles up the road from us. I wanted a home surrounded by a mix of trees, so I purchased young coconut tree sprouts, papayas for their seeds, breadnut and bread fruit trees, and even a couple kola nut tree plants for the yard. Soon, there were lines of young coconut trees along the borderline of our property, with papaya trees and young soursop trees growing everywhere on our property. I was young, in my early thirties, and dreaming of the days ahead when our children would be climbing up the trees I had planted. I dreamed of them running wild, falling up and down our steep yard, running from the edge of the yard at the swamp to the top of the hill where our home slants as though it might fall during a storm. I dreamed of days ahead when I would yell from the backdoor, calling my young children in for dinner, dreamed of the salty winds, blowing from the other side of the town, where the ocean waves rolled endlessly, the winds, careless.

My mother, Mary, otherwise known as Hne Dahtedor in our Grebo language, was a regular in our home, even though she did not permanently live with us. Mama, as I called her, must have been in her fifties then, but she was as strong as a rubber band. She would come during weekends or during the week when I needed her to help me out with the children. She loved to help me in the yard with my vegetable crops. I decided to make this home self-sufficient, so most days, when I was not at work teaching, I worked outside. I spent many days planting any vegetables we could consume, including sweet potatoes for their leaves, collard greens, eddoes or cocoyams, for their roots. Mama decided she would use a vacant front lot that belonged to a cousin of ours to grow cassavas for their leaves and the root crop. Soon, there was a huge cassava farm in front of our yard instead of the annoying unattended brush.

But I was not yet satisfied with just crops. I wanted to produce my own eggs and chickens, so my husband built a chicken coop in the backyard, and soon, I had chickens, ducks, and eggs. I was so self-sufficient; neighbors came to me for greens, for papayas, even water from our outdoor well. The guava and orange trees were not yet ready, but I could see my neighbors lining up someday to buy fresh fruits from me. Within a few months of moving into our home, you could stand in our yard and see dozens of chickens running freely.

When I needed to cook chicken for dinner, I would call my chickens to me. I had a call, "Kudu, kudu, kudu," that I trained them to know by first using the call as a dinner call. Soon, each rooster and hen and their chicks knew that this call meant there was food. Whenever I called, they would rush across the yard, leaping over brush and vegetables to come to me. Soon, they knew my voice, and did not come when another member of the household called them.

I fed them on rice cream powder I bought from the rice cleaning factory in the West Point market area. I had a mix of mostly Liberian free-range chickens with a few American breeds, and soon, I was getting a mix of different chicken breeds. I would call them for raw rice, something that chickens love, to peck at rice grains on the ground. When I needed chicken for dinner, I would use my call, and my brother Wyne, who lived with us, would snatch one of the roosters for dinner. My father in-law, Saade Wesley, who was spending a few days with us, was shocked one day when he saw me snatch a rooster after I'd called them. "What kind of woman did my son marry? You nurse them when they're ill, you feed them, and when you need one of them for dinner, you grab one," he said in Grebo.

If you thought my crazy homemaking was complete by the end of 1988, you were wrong. I needed more to make my home a lively place. We already had three watchdogs—Jumbo Jet, Midnight, and K-O. Our yard was protected only by a barbwire fence. The three dogs were therefore a terror to thieves with any intention to break in. Living in Liberia those days was difficult. The Liberian economy was failing fast as we slowly lost the powerful American dollar. Liberia is the only African country where the US dollar is legal tender. By the end of the year, the Liberian dollar was no longer one-to-one with the US dollar. With such a crumbling economy, the number of thieves in Monrovia multiplied. The three dogs were our protection. They barked ferociously at every sound in the day or night, and could kill, if you let them loose. So, we kept them tied down with a leash all day, and set them loose at night.

But we needed something domestic; pigs, I thought, pigs. One day, my husband walked over to our agriculture professor neighbor friend and purchased three female piglets and one male. Mlen-Too had already built me a pig pen to start my own business, or what I called a pig-raising hobby. Because our yard bordered the swamp, there were no houses behind us. Raising pigs in such a place was not a bad idea. With the help of family members, including my husband, I now had a lot more to do.

I often would drive out into the slums of West Point and purchase huge sacks of rice cream powder, not just for the chickens now, but also for the pigs. Then I'd drive to a couple supermarkets in downtown Monrovia for their rotten vegetables and fruits, and then to the bread bakeries near Monrovia's South Beach prison yard on the UN Drive to purchase sacks of expired bread from the baker. We supplemented all of this food supply with clover grass and wild vegetables from our neighborhood. Soon, our pigs were ready to give us more piglets.

And finally, I knew that we had built ourselves a place we could call home. Unlike my years of growing up on Capitol Hill with overcrowding houses and in a home, crowded by my stepmother's anger against her stepchildren, here, I could be free, could live my dream as a professor, writer, and a homemaker. This was home. This was not our original dream home, however. We had adopted a smaller plan than our original planned architecture of a colonial style home. We even abandoned our original two lots, located in Paynesville, for this beautiful island of rolling hills left here by God, along the Mesurado and the vast swampland.

But one day, all of that came under attack. In the early hours of December 24, 1989, in a small town close to the Liberian-Guinean border, Butuo in Nimba County, the Liberian warlord Charles Taylor and his rebels invaded and began the Liberian civil war. Soon, what I had dreamed of as home was under attack. On July 2, 1990, after six months of ravaging

Liberia, Charles Taylor's rebels captured Paynesville City, just a few miles up the road from our Congo Town home, and soon, bullets and missiles were flying around us. Soon, this lovely terrain of rolling hills was overrun by Taylor's rebels and government soldiers. And soon, we too, had to flee the random killings, the stray bullets and rockets landing in our neighborhood.

Soon, we and our chickens, our ducks, our pigs, even our dogs were in grave danger. The neighborhood that was once lively with screaming children, the sounds of salty winds from the ocean, the place with a rushing river at the back of our yard was threatened by war. Soon, thieves were breaking in at night and stealing the chickens and the pigs we had slaughtered only a few times before the onset of the war. One day in July, 1990, as the sounds of war raged around us, a Catholic priest and friend of ours, Rev. Andrew Momolue Diggs, pulled up into the yard in a truck amidst the now ghost town of Pagos Island. They needed pigs to feed refugees, and we quickly donated dozens of pigs to the Catholic Relief Services. Maybe this was why we had done all this work, I thought.

Soon, we had to flee home, joining the exodus of thousands out of Monrovia, into makeshift displaced refugee centers that were springing up around the country. Soon, what we called home was overrun by war and a bloodbath beyond human imagination, and in March of 1991, our family had to flee Liberia for the United States.

Today, that home is being renovated by our son, Mlen-Too II. Maybe I will one day live again in my home, the first home we built out of our meager salaries. There, in that history of my lost home and homeland, remains the beauty of the slanting Pagos

Island hills, the elusive river coming to my backyard from the Atlantic Ocean and returning in that cycle of life in a beautiful country where I still belong.

scars

PAUL MCVEIGH

oogle Earth is extraordinary. It's like looking into a crystal ball from a 1980's fantasy film. 'Take me to Jamaica Street,' I say. 'Take me home.' The pixelated mist clears and here it is.

What I see first is not our house but the view as though looking out our front window. If Google Earth could go back in time to my childhood (next update?) I'd see waste ground and old, crumbling, abandoned shells of houses where I used to play. If I could see snapshots on fast-forward from then to now, I'd see those ruins demolished to make room for a housing estate. Houses with indoor toilets and immersion heaters for hot water, seen as the height of luxury.

I read somewhere that the Ardoyne I knew was the 'biggest slum in Europe.' And if that wasn't enough, The Troubles were raging; riots, bombs, paramilitary parades, armed police and the British Army patrolling the streets with rifles.

That new housing estate was built on the waste ground to accommodate the ever growing Catholic population – 'breeding the Protestants out' was the joke and the threat. They were also to house the Catholics being burned out of their houses in other areas of the city.

Looking at the view from our front window now, there is a tiny square of garden dotted with some saplings, a little green heart at the centre of that estate.

Turning the viewer to my house is a shock. The house I grew up in has gone. Not a brick left. Replaced by a newer, bigger model. I don't know how I feel about that. It will take some time to absorb. Apart from this small block of upgraded houses, my street looks the same as I remember when leaving it for good, in 1987, to go to university. I'm laughing to myself; the last time I went to my childhood home, I had made the trip down from Portstewart where I lived while attending the University of Ulster at Coleraine. In my hand, a suitcase full of dirty washing for my Mum to do. I knocked at number 52 to find a stranger answering the door. My parents had moved without telling me. The look on that woman's face as she told me where to find my family.

This is not as strange as it sounds. In those days having a home phone was a bit of a luxury. I didn't have one in Portstewart and didn't call home that often from the phone box on the promenade because I was too busy soaking up university life. Besides, my parents were awkward on the phone, particularly my mother, who seemed to be frightened of it somehow.

I'm surprised how, for the most part, Jamaica Street is the same as I left it twenty-eight years ago when, while growing up, our part of the street changed so dramatically. Partly due to the slum clearance but also because in the 1970's, in Belfast, buildings were burned, bombed, looted and left for dead, just like the people who lived and worked in them. Often the scars these buildings left on the ground were the only proof they'd ever existed.

The Troubles. It is a weak name given to that period of time. It doesn't suggest terror. The Troubles doesn't conjure the oppression, the fear, the physical danger you had to negotiate to get to the local shop, your friend's house or, on one occasion, this occasion I recall, getting to school.

I was only late for school once in my life. I don't remember the reason for my lateness that day but I know I was never late again. I was eleven. No longer in Holy Cross Boys' Primary School at the bottom of my street, I now had to go up the Crumlin Road into a Protestant area to get to St. Gabriel's Secondary School.

That day, I walked behind our house, across more waste ground, covered in glass from petrol bombs and milk bottles thrown during riots. Past the Highfield Club. This was an ugly box where men went to drink. The whole building was encompassed by a metal cage. In order to get in you had to buzz the gate. If you were let inside there was further security at the door. This was because paramilitaries on both sides took to bursting into bars and clubs, letting go with their guns, killing many of those trapped inside.

As I take this journey now, Google Earth shows the area is a back road, neatly surfaced, no bumps or glass and no trace left of the Highfield.

I walked through the gap in the houses to Etna Drive that morning and up through the terraced houses of Ardoyne. This all looks much the same except there aren't as many political slogans and rousing quotes painted on the walls.

'Ireland unfree shall never be at peace'

'Our Day Will Come!'

'It is not those that inflict the most but those that endure the most shall win'

Powerful stuff that many miles and many years haven't erased.

On the Ardoyne Road I look down to the now permanent protest at Woodvale roundabout started in 2013. British Flags stand proud, banners and signs of support from Protestant communities to mark their anger at the ruling that prevented their marching bands from parading down this Catholic part of the road.

Straight ahead I see Ardoyne Library is still there. The shutters are down and I fear the worst. A quick Google search for 'Ardoyne Library opening times' shows it's still in business. Thank God. I would hide in there, in books, every day after school, away from the violence of the streets. With the Woodvale protest just yards away there may still be things kids from Ardoyne want to hide from.

To get to St. Gabriel's, my new secondary school, I had to turn right and walk up the Crumlin Road. The further you went up, the more Protestant it became. The Irish flags on lampposts and Republican slogans on walls were swapped for British Union Jacks and Unionist slogans. One remains branded in my mind: *'Kill All Taigs!'*

Taigs meant Catholics. *Taigs* meant me.

I had to walk past two Protestant secondary schools—one for boys, the other for girls. In Northern Ireland schools weren't just segregated by religion but gender too, though some Protestants schools mixed—never Catholic. God forbid! The schools along the Crumlin Road had staggered start times to avoid clashes. Being late for school didn't just mean getting into trouble with your teacher or being sent to the headmaster, it also meant you were in real danger.

Everton Girls' School has now become the Everton Centre for community health services. On the day I was late, I walked past there first and saw no one. But halfway between Everton and my school a group of boys came from Hesketh Road and stared at me. Coming from that road meant they were Protestant. If I hadn't been wearing my school uniform I could have tried lying. We would practice what to say if we were ever caught. Like spies with false identities, we'd have a new name, address and backstory. Your name usually gave away your religion—being Irish, or an obvious Saint. Your address—the areas were segregated so that gave you away too. A few quick questions usually uncovered the truth—the local football team you supported, for example. The letter 'H' was a shibboleth. Protestant schools taught the pronunciation as 'aitch' and the Catholic schools taught 'haitch.' Crazy to think a slip of the tongue, the pronunciation of a consonant, could lead to your death.

But as I was on my way to school there was no hiding, my uniform was like a national flag.

I turned back and ran. But I was small for my age and the boys gained on me fast. Some older girls came out of the Everton school gates now in front of me. I was trapped. I had no choice but to run out in front of the traffic on the main road. I tripped and fell, my school bag burst open and my books scattered over the road. The cars drove around me, over my books. None stopped. Adults. Scared or uncaring. The boys surrounded me and dragged me by the legs and arms along the road cheering. On the pavement they kicked and punched. I knew what was going to happen. I knew what had happened to the young man who lived a few doors from me, caught and dragged to a building site where they dropped breeze blocks on his head. This was not an urban myth. I saw his coffin carried out of his house.

I closed my eyes and curled up in a ball.

I heard girls shouting. The beating stopped. I opened my eyes to see the group of girls pulling the boys away. I don't remember what they said as they circled me but the anger of the boys was directed away from me and the girls took it. They were fearless. Arms picked me up. More girls arrived and stopped the traffic, collecting my books and bag from the road. They walked me to school. Keeping the boys back. They fixed my tie. They tidied my hair. Soothed me. Cuddled me. Apologised. They were ashamed. I know now I wouldn't have ended up dead, but I didn't then. Who knows how far they would have gone? But I had been saved by the same 'people' who attacked me. I had everything I'd ever been told about Protestants confirmed and dismantled in the same experience. I had to rebuild my understanding, find a new way to think.

The best weapons against hatred and violence have always been courage and humanity and the battlefields are the hearts and minds of your enemy.

As I turn my viewer, Google Earth shows me St. Gabriel's Secondary School has gone, just like the house I grew up in. Only here, nothing has replaced it. It has now become just like the waste ground I'd see from the window of our house as a boy. All that's left to prove it was ever there is this gap in the street and the scars it's left behind on the Earth.

classic six

JULIE METZ

I t's my building, the one I grew up in, incorrectly numbered on tree-lined West End Avenue, Manhattan, New York City, USA, Google Earth. This was my mother's adopted neighborhood, just down the street from the apartment where she lived with her parents shortly after their flight from Nazi-occupied Vienna in 1940. German and Yiddish were spoken on these streets then, and in so many apartments where Jewish refugees had found sanctuary. My father, a Philadelphian, child of Russian immigrants who fled a previous wave of anti-Semitic persecution in the Ukraine, met my mother on a blind date in 1947 and happily left his own city for life in Manhattan. He and my mother moved to this building when I was a year old, having outgrown their one-bedroom apartment down the street.

Elegant green canopy outside, installed after I left for college when gentrification moved uptown in a hurry, evicting the residents of the single room occupancy hotels on the side streets, loitering impatiently until folks in rent-controlled apartments croaked or moved to Brooklyn or fled to the suburbs. Above the canopy, a pre-war apartment building of fifteen floors (superstitiously skipping unlucky 13), with a white façade at street level, brown brick above, every pore of baked clay infused with decades of city soot and grime. The fifth floor has the sweet Juliet terraces, too small to use, even to gaze at the inconstant moon. The architect's style is some 1920s mash-up of nineteenth-century grandeur by way of Medieval Castle Revival. When I count up to the sixth floor I see the air conditioning units in my father's apartment windows. More recent apartment co-op buyers have installed central air. The Street View photo shows bright yellow compactors and street pavers parked in front of the building in the sparse shade of young trees. What a racket that must have made as workers jackhammered and removed street asphalt to replace a section of water pipe or sewer, layer upon layer, excavating the hidden cobblestones that once paved the avenue. I recall my dad and his wife complaining bitterly about the noise. Spring, summer, or autumn in New York City is always about street work, your block or a neighbor's, ancient infrastructure in a continuous state of near collapse.

West End Avenue, my home. Rumble of cars on well-worn granite cobblestones is the continuous white noise background to our lives. An opera singer rehearses in her apartment across the avenue, her scales and arias trilling into our open windows —*ah-ah-ah-AH-ah-ah-ah!*—rancid perfume of uncollected trash wafts upward from the back courtyard in summer—*Ah-ah-ah-AH-ah-ah-ah!*—honking horns on Broadway, one avenue over, where my mother shops at Sloan's and the green grocer and Harry, the German butcher, one of the only times I hear her speak her first language. When fire trucks race down the avenue with sirens blaring, my younger brother Simon is nearly desperate with excitement, pressing his hands and freckled nose against the windowpanes for a better look. *Don't!* My mother shouts for the umpteenth time. *Don't lean on the window!* Summertime, hair damp from the playground sprinklers in Riverside Park, where under the watchful eye of Hortense, our babysitter, Simon and I strip down to our white underwear and run through the cold spray. The old ladies sitting outside in folding chairs never fail to squish our cheeks when we return, paying special attention to Simon, with his dark curls and thick glasses. These crinkly ladies suffocate us with hair spray, talcum powder, and rose perfume. In winter Hortense waits for us outside the building as we are released from the school bus, bundled in swishing jackets and snowpants, mitten strings tugging and rubbing inside our sleeves.

Through heavy glass doors, up the stairs into the dimly lit lobby, where handsome Victor and portly Albert stand sentry in their gray uniforms, sorting the mail. Dark carved wood chairs in the lobby which we aren't allowed to sit in and creak when we do. Off to the right, the ornate wood-paneled manual elevator for our side of the building. If no one else is going upstairs, Victor lets us work the polished brass lever up to the sixth floor. Our apartment is on the right side as you step out of the elevator. The lock is tricky—you have to jiggle the keys just so. Inside, our hallway is dark, lined with bookshelves, and the parquet floors creak spooky-like.

Two bedrooms, each with white-tiled bathrooms. A maid's room, big enough for a twin bed for when Hortense sleeps over. L-shaped kitchen, painted shiny marigold yellow, my mother's domain when the lights are on. Cockroaches rule at night. She grunts as she smushes them with her bare palm if she goes in there after the dishes are done. My dad uses the dining room as his artist's studio. We can watch him through the glass doors but we aren't supposed to disturb him. He listens to music while he works, or sometimes a baseball game. He uses clam-shells we find in Maine for his paint palettes. The living room is furnished with low couch, coffee table, credenza, dining table and chairs. It is a room rarely used, except when my parents host dinner parties and during the hours I spend after school doing battle with the upright piano. A series of Japanese wood-cut prints hangs on the wall: landscapes of mountains, figures in pointed hats hurrying across a bridge in the rain. One is of a Samurai warrior dressed in an ornate black robe, wielding a sword against an unseen enemy, a fearsome companion who stares me down as I practice.

The two bedrooms face West End Avenue. My brother and I share one of them. The wood floor is covered with black and white speckled linoleum where we pile our stacks of wooden blocks, Lego creations and race Simon's Matchbox cars. Our twin beds are on opposite sides of the room. In the middle is a low round table set under the overhead light where we draw pictures, play board games, or arrange tea parties for stuffed animals and my dress-up dolls. We are not allowed to play in the hallway, we are not allowed to throw balls or jump around. But the room is our place, where I am mostly the boss of our games. Until Simon whacks me with a school book bag because he is tired of me being the boss. Until my mother stands in the doorway and says *clean up this room right now*, and then the magic force field is gone and it's time for dinner.

My mother works in midtown at the same publishing company as my father. We only get to visit their office on school vacations. They come home from work on the Riverside Drive bus at six o'clock, after Underdog and Rocky & Bullwinkle. We watch them on the black and white Zenith in our room. When my parents get home, my father changes out of his suit and shirt and tie and goes to his painting studio. My mother makes dinner. The best is when she takes out the electric pan, which means we are having fried chicken. If she is making liver I nearly puke from the smell, but we have to eat everything because there are children starving in Biafra. Sometimes I can hide bits in a napkin and then throw them away when no one is looking. My mother is tired, so that helps. She irons my dad's shirts after dinner while we go back to our room for a bath and bedtime.

The room changes at night, even when we are still awake. Sometimes we listen to a man telling a Just-So Story on our record player, in a rich voice I recognize from the Christmastime Grinch movie, while we look at the pictures in our book. I know the pictures by heart. I lie in bed mulling over the Elephant's Child's 'satiable curtiosity' and the Parsee's cake that made the rhinoceros's skin itch into wrinkles until my parents turn out the overhead light and say goodnight. There is still plenty of light from the outside world—the street lights on West End Avenue and the car headlights flashing beams across our ceiling, and always that rumbling, like approaching ocean waves, louder and louder till they pass under our window, then quiet again until the next one passes. The room is an island surrounded by waves, and then it is three small islands—my brother and me in our beds, and the smaller island of the round table under the ceiling light where my mother puts The Vaporizor—a machine that looks like a sightless white duck with a curved bill—that blows out cold mist at night so my brother can breathe better. The Vaporizor shushes other sounds, like my parents getting ready for bed in the other room, but it can never shush the waves outside our window, even in the winter.

I wake in the night. The black-robed samurai warrior wielding his sword flies away into his white paper world, but I am all sweaty, wedged between teddy bear and dolls. A car rumbles down the avenue, then the street is quiet, just the hum of the Vaporizer. The three white glass globes of the ceiling light stare down at me. I never noticed that the globes form the triangle of a face, milky eyes and gaping mouth, and I never noticed the wispy aura around the globes. I get out of bed and tiptoe over to The Vaporizer, placing my hands in front of its open mouth to feel the cool mist. I close my eyes and put my face into the blast of damp wind. It's like the seaspray mist kicked up by the passenger ferry we take to the Maine island in the summer. If I keep my eyes closed I can pretend I'm there. When I open them again and look up the white globes are still staring at me, expressionless but menacing, like the empty eye sockets of a skull. I scurry back to bed and burrow under the sheets and blankets. Teddy and dolls will guard my island. It's hot and airless under the covers. I worry that I might suffocate. I slide just the top of my head into the night air, keeping my eyes squeezed shut. When I peek, the lamp is still staring down at me. Maybe it isn't fair to make Teddy and dolls do all the work. I pull them under the covers and slide the rest of my head out. I will stand guard. I will defend my island against all invaders, including Samurai warriors and the ghost in the overhead lamp. I fold an arm across my closed eyes so that I won't be tempted to look up at the face above me.

I wake in the morning with my arm still across my eyes, stiff and numb as if it doesn't belong to my body at all. The arm wakes up tingling with pins and needles and then it becomes my arm again. The room is my room, my brother is across the room in his bed. Classical music is playing loudly on the radio in the hall. I can smell toast burning in the kitchen. Another school day.

My eye scans down the building to the street, and the yellow construction equipment parked in front of the building. I wonder how often the photos change. Next time the camera passes by, the yellow equipment will be gone and the street will look as it does when I visit my father, now ninety, and his second wife. Victor and Albert are long gone, but there is still one doorman, Jose, who smiles with recognition when I walk into the lobby, still ersatz Medieval, the wooden lobby chairs replaced with contemporary designs. The manual elevator is automatic, the original wood interior refinished and gleaming. Upstairs, my father and his wife serve us lunch in the living room, rearranged and brightened since my mother's death almost ten years ago. The floors are sanded and varnished a pale oak, the walls are white instead of maroon. Even the marigold yellow kitchen is now white. The roaches have been beaten back. A new table has replaced the Formica one my mother used to prepare and serve our meals. My father's wife uses the bedroom my brother and I shared as an office, with the same ceiling fixture. The paned windows have been replaced with airtight single pane modernity. I greet the Samurai warrior in the living room. Every time I visit, my father and his wife ask me to take away something—dishes, silverware, books. They are lightening their load.

Sometimes I pace these rooms where I played as a child and brooded as an adolescent, looking for objects I know are long gone—our play table and chairs, The Vaporizer. I open the closet in my old bedroom half expecting to see a familiar coat or dress. Sometimes I scan the rooms with the appraising eye of an eager real estate agent, wondering who will live here next. Not me again, I am sure of that, not in these six rooms. *Classic Six Co-op in elegant prewar building, Upper West Side. All new windows, EIK, original parquet floors, bathrooms, and period details, near great public schools, Riverside Park, shopping, transportation. Bring your architect and make it your own!* I snap back quickly to my present comfort—that my father can live his remaining years here with his books and music and art. In his bedroom I visit with the photos of my mother perched on the dresser. I think she would like the changes my dad and his wife have made, though she didn't embrace change as a rule. Before I leave, I peek out the window to West End Avenue and draw a finger through the fine layer of city dust settled on the windowsill, rubbing the black pigment between my fingers like a balm.

smile when you say that

ELLEN MEISTER

'm not a slow-witted person, but I've never been very good at responding to insults. When someone says something passive-aggressive, like, "You know, I really admire you for having resisted getting a nose job," or "I wish I had the courage to wear that dress," I usually just blink in confusion while processing their intention. Sarcasm, too, takes a circuitous route to my frontal lobe. If you were to say, "Way to get to the point, Meister. Your essay is rocking my world," I'd likely utter a weak "Thanks," while trying to decide if you were serious. And condescension is the worst, because I immediately feel it in my bones, yet freeze in place. Or even smile politely. An hour later, after the offender has blithely wandered off and forgotten about me, I'm left furious ... mostly at myself for not having throttled the jerk.

The good news is that I'm a writer, which means I can exact revenge at any time in the future by putting the culprit in a story. Or in this case, an essay.

Indulge me, because I have to start this particular tale at the beginning. The very beginning. So cue the violins. Or rather, cue the whole damned string section. I'll need it to garner your sympathy. Because if you did a Google Earth search on the house I grew up in, you would see a lovely suburban home in a privileged neighborhood. And if Google Earth had a time machine, you'd witness a scene that looks like something out of *The Wonder Years*, complete with loving parents.

And yet I was a wretched little bugger. At home, my bullying older brother made my life unbearable. And school was even worse. I simply couldn't figure out how to fit in, and I wallowed in the muck at the bottom of the social strata, teased and picked on.

The teachers weren't much better. My memory isn't perfect, but I'm ninety-nine percent sure my fifth grade science and math classes were taught by Lucretia Borgia.

Now cut the string section and cue the flutophone, because here's the happy part. All I had to do to escape my misery was hang in there long enough to graduate high school. In college I blossomed, discovering that I wasn't necessarily an unworthy mass of drain sludge, and that once the forces of evil were peeled away, I actually had a naturally cheerful (if understandably anxious) disposition.

I also had a strong survival instinct, because I broke the pattern of my past by marrying a sweet and darling man who thinks I'm a goddess of talent, beauty, grace and back rubs. And he doesn't insult me. In fact, he never misses a chance to pay me a compliment.

Yeah, people find us nauseating.

But we procreated all the same. While living in our first

apartment, we had one son and then another. Soon, our lovely pre-war condo started to feel a little crowded, so we decided it was time to move to the suburbs and give the children the chance to grow up with a yard and a first-class public school education.

But anxiety over my past went to war with my hope for the future, because we were house-shopping on Long Island, where I grew up. It was the natural place for us to live, since our parents and siblings were still there and we wanted to be among family. Besides, my brother and I were getting along better. He had stopped bullying me and turned his harassment to the world at large. In other words, he became a lawyer. And a Republican.

I quelled the anxiety by insisting that we avoid the town where I grew up. So we instructed our realtor to show us homes that were north, south, east and west of my old neighborhood. It was like circling a drain, and the longer we looked for a house, the closer we got to being sucked in.

Like most couples, my husband and I had a list of criteria for our home. We wanted a colonial, not a split-level. We wanted a deep backyard. We wanted an exceptional school district. We wanted a house we could afford.

But months of looking yielded no results. The houses were either too expensive or had the wrong layout. We tried under-bidding on properties outside our budget and were turned down. We kept searching, and as the choices thinned our hopes were diminished. One day, I complained to my younger sister about the problem.

"I don't think we'll ever find the home we're looking for," I said, despondent.

"That's because you're an idiot," she replied.

"Oh?" I retorted.

Little sister went on to explain that my stubbornness was getting in the way of my family's future, as the town we grew up in had everything I was looking for in a home. And besides, Lucretia Borgia had retired and moved to Florida. And the kids who had tormented me had grown up and moved out.

Still, I resisted. And then it happened. My husband discovered an ad for a house that had everything we wanted... smack in the middle of my old neighborhood. Weakened, I agreed to look at it, assuring him I would not want to live there.

But when I stepped into the sunny colonial, everything changed. The heavens parted. The angels sang. It was the very house we had been looking for. It was home.

So even though it was only blocks from my childhood address, we bought it. That was eighteen years ago, and I quickly grew confident we had made the right decision. My fears melted away as my painful memories were replaced with the joys of motherhood and the focus of making sure my kids were healthy and happy.

Then the past beckoned in the form of an invitation to a high school reunion. To my delight, I discovered I had no worries about facing my classmates. Too many years had passed. I had grown comfortable in my skin and felt confident in myself. Besides, my classmates had matured, too. There was nothing to worry about.

There was just one small twinge of apprehension that accompanied me as I approached the venue. What would people think of me for moving back to the old town? Would they judge me as small-minded, provincial and simply too dull to imagine a world outside of our hometown?

Nonsense, I told myself. That's your insecure inner child coming back to haunt you. You are a grown woman, a published author. People will treat you with dignity and respect.

And I was right, they did. So I let my guard down. I connected with old friends. I had fun.

I walked right up to our old valedictorian and asked about his life. He asked about mine. I told him where I lived.

"My dear," he said, "that's utterly pathetic."

"Wait. What?"

"I mean, why be so provincial, so limited, so small-minded? Don't you know there's a whole wide world outside our hometown?"

"Um ..."

"Excuse me," he said. "I see someone I really want to talk to."

And then he walked away, leaving me standing there, holding my drink and feeling like Mrs. Borgia had just handed me back a test with a D-. I was crushed. Demoralized. Worst of all, I had smiled at him to the very end, as if I were the luckiest girl in the world, so enriched was I by the wisdom of his words.

Next time, heaven help me, I'll think of a snappy comeback —something that will cut the offender like a sharpened blade. It will be brilliant, witty, eviscerating. I'll say it right to his face. I'll say it without a moment of hesitation. And the acid of my remark will be powerful enough to melt the very flesh from his bones.

Or maybe I'll just write another essay.

commonwealth

PAMELA ERENS

My childhood in Chicago in the 1960s and 1970s coincided with a nadir in American urban life. If Chicago, unlike New York City, didn't go bankrupt, it suffered from the same rise in drug use and crime, the same deterioration of public facilities and public manners, the same graffiti and unsafe subways and angry gloom. In my memories, Chicago has a wholly muted palette: the gray of stone, the tan of brick, with a faint scrim of grime over the whole. I surrendered my citizenship to the place when I turned sixteen. My last two years of high school were spent at boarding school in New Hampshire, and after that, I remained on the East Coast, home only for parts of summers and some holidays.

We lived near the lake: vast Lake Michigan, whose opposite shore was never visible. It might have been the ocean. I didn't know that most urban children don't grow up within walking distance of miles of beach. Granted, that beach was filthy, full of alewives that washed up onto the sand and rotted there, stinking and giving me nightmares about stepping on their open eyes. Still, a family could take a Sunday afternoon and

71

spread out a blanket in the sand, eat a picnic, make dirty castles. My little brother and I ran just as far as the lake edge, longing to splash in the waves but forbidden from going into the toxic waters. "You could get sick," my mother told us, so we gazed at the one or two reckless bathers in the distance and then carefully watched our feet as we zigzagged back to our parents' side.

To say we lived near the lake, and to add that we lived on the North Side, adjacent to the seven-mile stretch of Lincoln Park, is to say that we lived on a thin rind of affluence, in many ways segregated from the rest of the city. To simplify, Chicago consists of only three cardinal points on the compass: north, south, and west. East is the lake. The closer to the lake, the ritzier, generally, the real estate. (One North Side neighborhood is actually called the Gold Coast.) After their marriage, my father, a lawyer and the first in his family to go to college, and my mother, a Washington, D.C., transplant, lived in a high-rise apartment on Lake Shore Drive; after I arrived, we moved into another high-rise apartment on a street called Lakeview. When I was six we made a final move into a duplex slightly farther north. I cried terribly when I learned of this move, but warmed up when I discovered I would be getting my own bedroom, and when I saw the features of the 1920s building that would be our new home. The entrance looked like a medieval castle. The exterior double doors, of yellow oak, had three panels each of opaque glass shaped into Gothic peaks, and were recessed into a massive stone archway with blind tracery. To each side of the doors were lanterns of yellow glass encased in filigreed and oxidized copper or bronze. Google Earth shows me these images, twenty years after I last saw them, with great fidelity. Even at six

I could see that whoever drew up the plans for this facade, whoever did the stone carvings, had made a great and heavy beauty. Entering the small, slate-tiled foyer in my navy school jumper and white blouse, I would be wrapped in a sudden coolness and dimness, as if I had entered the heart of a fairy tale. Inside the apartment were more wonders: a living room two stories high with wrought-iron balconies, a bedroom with a four-poster bed and tall windows looking out over the park and the sun-struck water from fourteen floors up. When I stood near them I felt I was floating.

The Chicago I lived in for sixteen years was bounded by the Loop—the oldest section of downtown—to the south, Clark and Halsted Streets to the west (a triangle where I could shop, when I was older, at Barbara's Bookstore and the funky health-food shop, and where "the gay neighborhood" began), and Foster Avenue to the north, where my orthodontist was. Children accept their circumstances as natural and correct, but even then I understood that there were other Chicagos that looked very different from my own. I watched the TV news, and read the newspaper from a young age, and it seemed as if every few weeks there was some sort of public school strike. The idea of children not going to school was upsetting to me, a school-lover. It conjured up images of kids shut up in dark, deserted rooms or throwing rocks in the street. (I don't know where those images came from. A radio report?) In the evenings on Channel 9 there were people hurried in ambulances with flashing lights to hospitals after shootings. These things happened "west" or "south," especially south. On the South Side were the traditionally black neighborhoods; the West Side was (in my understanding) white people, but white people who had Polish last names and worked out of trucks and drank beer and lived in two- or three-story multifamily houses with outside stairs between levels. I knew this because after my mother enrolled in graduate school we sometimes visited school friends of hers who lived in such houses. I was always vaguely uncomfortable—even resentful—in these homes, which felt cramped and shabby to me. Why didn't these friends clean the bathrooms better? Why wasn't there anyplace nice to sit? The answer clearly had something to do with money (although a certain bohemianism was also mixed in), a subject my family almost never spoke of. Without being told, I understood that it was embarrassing to do so, gauche.

What I knew about the South Side I knew because of our black housekeeper, and it was vanishingly little. I was eleven when she came to work for us; she was in her late fifties. Juanita was neither substitute parent nor faceless employee. She was a small, warm, gentle woman in a white uniform who delighted me by calling me "Baby" in her Arkansas-inflected accent. Occasionally I sat in her room off the kitchen, chatting or watching detective shows with her. For all the thousands of hours she spent in our apartment (she slept over part of every week, and continued working for my family until I was in my mid twenties), I never once set foot in hers, or even in her neighborhood. It would never have occurred to me, or to my parents, to suggest such a visit. I knew that Juanita sometimes went with her friends on weekends to jazz or blues clubs, but that was almost the only glimpse of her life outside of our home that she gave me. I probably didn't exhibit too much curiosity. One day, however, I learned that she had been held up at gunpoint in the vestibule of her building as she returned there from work. She told me that she had hesitated to turn over her purse, which contained her week's pay. I remember finding this puzzling: of course you would give up your purse for your life! A no-brainer! But Juanita insisted: "It was hard. It was very hard."

The only other time Juanita's Chicago was invoked was a few years later, when I was in college and one of her five grand-children, a teenager, was shot dead in what appeared to be a drug-related dispute. I phoned her to express my condolences and, surprising me again, she said that her grandson "had gotten involved in things he shouldn't have." She did not say this with anguish or anger but as if to indicate that the world ran on certain principles, and if those principles were violated, certain consequences might be expected. I wondered at her philosophical tone. I know that she was religious; maybe that helped her manage her grief. It's also possible that she did not want to inflict that grief on me, someone she continued to see as a child for whose welfare she was responsible.

So that was Chicago: gold along the lake—light-filled apartments, the Lincoln Park Zoo and botanical gardens, bike paths and beaches, the Art Institute and the elegant Water Tower shopping mall—monotony and grit to the west, and fear and violence to the south.

Naturally it was more complicated than that. I am talking about the divisions I absorbed as a child and teenager. There was the Chicago I spent most of my time in, and then there was what felt to me like a pre-existing, larger, in some ways realer Chicago: the leached-of-color, noisy, neon-lighted city slightly outside my orbit in both space and time. My grandparents' jewelry store in the Loop, on the tenth floor of a retail-wholesale building with endless hallways of tan linoleum. Its exotic back room—manila boxes with handwritten labels, scratch pads with the intricate scrollwork of the store logo on them—where my brother and I were allowed to play while business went on. The gruff, big-bellied, almost always male customers, representatives of a generation one step closer to Eastern Europe and the Jewish communities my grandparents' parents had fled for greater opportunity or greater safety. A generation that was only sparsely educated but that would educate its own. My great-uncle, wreathed in cigar smoke, who made a great show of bestowing a five-dollar bill on my brother each time he visited our home. The El, with its deafening rattle, casting dark shadows on the commercial enterprises below; the tall towers of the Cabrini Green projects seen from our car en route to the expressway; the outdoor flea market of Maxwell Street, where I got my wallet stolen at fifteen. I was unnerved by this, the first time I was personally touched by a crime, and learned a valuable lesson—don't carry your wallet in the back pocket of your corduroys. My mother and father were resigned. "People around there are poor," they said, framing the theft more as a *Les Miz* bread-stealing type of event than as the canny seizing of an opportunity. There were hints of the "realer" Chicago even from my bedroom window, for in addition to the park and the lake, the view revealed the tops of the nearest buildings, with their functional accoutrements: water towers, smoke stacks, unidentifiable receptacles and piping.

This idea of a real Chicago was and is romance, of course. My life of private school and upscale shopping was no less real than lives lived among the city's car dealerships or trash-strewn lots. The romance was probably heightened by Chicago's striking class segregation. When I first started spending a good bit of time in New York City (moving there when I was twenty-four), the life of its streets felt much more mixed than I was used to. This was probably even more true in 1988 than now, when great swaths of affluence have returned to the city. In most neighborhoods I encountered people with money and people without, suit-and-tie types and punks, black and white (and Asian and Hispanic), brain workers and brawn workers, dirt and art. People of all classes rode the subway (I'd never once ridden the El in Chicago, nor did my parents ever do so). This kind of city life felt comfortable, and exhilarating, as if the two sides of my upbringing had merged at last: the side I knew well, and its only-glimpsed shadow twin. As if I had always been waiting for an existence that was a little messier, a little more chaotic, than the one I'd been raised into. In New York, I lived in small spaces, sometimes along with cockroaches and mice, and walked to work through the tatty stretches of Chinatown and the Bowery. My office, at a weekly news and culture magazine, was beyond dingy, with big carpet stains and ceiling insulation that was coming down. It was a bit of a gamble walking from there to the subway after late hours. To be sure, I always had the resources to avoid drastically unsafe places, and the shabbiness I enjoyed was the shabbiness of the arty liberal-left: that of editors and writers who like to feel that words and ideas matter more than material niceties. (I was beginning to understand those grad-student messy bathrooms after all.) But it was a relief to see a certain amount of life's disorder out in the open, not separated from me by the screen of a TV. I was old enough by that point to have become aware of the disorder in myself—the aggressions and resentments; the hormone-driven longings; the desperate desire to be noticed, to make a mark, whether a beautiful or ugly one—and maybe I needed to live in a place that reflected this disorder back at me more routinely.

I am always surprised when I return to Chicago every couple of years to see family. My parents and my brother still live there, although the apartment with the wonderful Gothic entranceway was given up long ago. The city looks brighter, cleaner, and more colorful than I remember. To a great degree it is cleaner and more colorful. The lake has gone through detox —the alewives are gone, and you can swim in the waters. There is Millennium Park, a gorgeous reclamation of space that used to be the abandoned railway tracks I would see from my grandmother's apartment window. Restaurants downtown are bursting with life, and Michigan Avenue is a canyon of tourist activity: American Girl, Hershey's, The Disney Store, Michael Kors. There's the new Museum of Contemporary Art, the carnival of Navy Pier. Again like other cities, Chicago has been "coming back" since the mid-nineties, with infusions of money and civic pride. I enjoy its newfound energy, but it's a different city, one I'm not intimate with. I know too that beyond downtown are other neighborhoods—Englewood, North Lawndale—that remain among the most violent in the country. The city I know, really know, is neither the city that existed during my childhood nor the one that exists now. It's a city of my imagination: glossy and frictionless, yet also coarse and threatening. It's the fantasy city of a protected child imagining what life will be like when she gets outside the castle. What might be waiting for her, the complications she can intuit but not yet inhabit.

home is for
the hard

JEFFERY RENARD ALLEN

I spent my first seven years in the neighborhood of Kenwood on Chicago's Southside, living under the care and protection of my mother in an apartment on the top floor of a three-story yellow brick courtyard building only a few blocks from the University of Chicago. In fact, my mother gave birth to me at the university's Wiley's Children's Hospital, but, located in the liberal yet all white enclave of Hyde Park, the university was worlds away from us.

Kenwood was a dangerous place to live in the late sixties, rife with poverty, crime, and gang violence. Notably, the neighborhood was the stomping grounds of the Blackstone Rangers, a street gang who took advantage of the times and refashioned themselves as the nationalist Black P Stone Nation, a clever con that allowed them to pocket government money earmarked for community organizations, money they used to buy guns and drugs and increase their stranglehold. Most of the black Southside bordering the university appeared uninhab-

79

itable—especially after the 1968 riots that followed Dr. Martin Luther King's assassination—an alien landscape of vacant lots, run-down buildings, and liquor stores and storefront churches festering on almost every corner.

The apartment I shared with my mother was overrun with mice. But that apartment was a constant source of fascination for me. Ghosts walked about during the middle of the night. In fact, I was on friendly terms with a spectral couple, man and wife, who dressed in nineteenth century garb. The daylight hours were equally wondrous. I would gaze out the windows into the sky, where on more than one occasion I saw a saucer of bright flickering lights, a mission-bound UFO. I also retain a vivid memory of gazing out the window and seeing King Kong climb up the facade of the Baptist church across the street. I watched Kong climb all the way to the top of the steeple. No way I will ever forget that.

But those otherworldly days came to an end one spring morning in 1969 as my mother walked me to school. She excitedly informed me that we would be moving to a new neighborhood, South Shore, later that day. When school was out, she would pick me up as usual, then we would make our way to South Shore.

Fearing that I would be left behind, I went home on my lunch break, to my mother's surprise and consternation. And that was that. Most of the physical details about the relocation have been lost to memory, but I can still hear the joyous sound of Stevie Wonder's "My Cherie Amour" that marked my entry into our new home, a third-floor apartment at 1828 East 72nd Street.

Bordering on Lake Michigan, South Shore was nothing

like Kenwood. It was a black neighborhood but it was not the ghetto, this soft and safe neighborhood of well-kept apartment buildings, two-flats, and one-family houses positioned on neat green streets with leafy trees and trim lawns and manicured backyards. Everyone held down a job, although the residents were mostly the working poor like my mother or middle class strugglers like the car mechanic who lived with his family in the apartment under ours. But South Shore had luxury in abundance too, namely one pristine area near the lakefront that sparkled with expansive and extravagant houses and mansions, where some celebrities like jazz great Ramsey Lewis lived.

In South Shore business thrived along 71st Street. My mother and I often went for hamburgers at the Woolworth's lunch counter, or had egg foo young, pepper steak, and shrimp fried rice at the Chinese take out, which is how I taught myself to use chopsticks. And tasty pizza (sausage and cheese) could be had at Reggio's, where at age nineteen I worked for minimum wage one summer scrubbing the wood-paneled freezer and shaping and flattening dough into pies.

My mother often sent me for groceries at the Jewish-owned supermarket. The ritual demanded that I bring our purchases to one good-hearted cashier, a heavyset light-skinned woman about my mother's age who knew that my mother struggled to make ends meet. Doing her part, she would slip a loaf of bread or package of ground beef or quart of milk into the brown paper bag without ringing up the items on her register.

Many Saturdays, I went with friends to the Jeffery Theater, where you could watch a double feature for one dollar. We preferred the Jeffery over the Hamilton, another movie house farther east on 71st Street, since word had it that hungry dog-sized rats hid inside the theater's dark smelly interiors. The times when we did go there we took the necessary precautions and would keep our feet elevated above the sticky floor through the duration of the movies.

Swimming at the YMCA on 71st Street was also high on the list of things to do. But we spent most of our time in the "alley," a large driveway between the building where I lived and the adjacent building. It was not an alley proper since the would-be thoroughfare ran several hundred feet from the street only to come to an abrupt end at a fenced-in grassy lot. The men would wash their cars here and perform mechanical work on bodies and engines, and they would also clean their campers and boats, air out their fishing and hunting gear, ready pails of worms or grease rifles. I envied the sons of these men because I longed to fish and hunt but I had no father.

Nefarious activity too. A dope dealer lived in the adjacent building and often conducted his business in plain view of everyone in the alley. Pimp-suited men would drive up in expensive cars and hand him bags of cash out the window. The cops tried to take him down with a late-night raid, but by the time they had broken through the steel gates on his doors and shot dead his German Shepherds, he had flushed all the dope down the toilet.

He remained on constant guard from that night on. Once I happened upon him in the alley, only for him to freeze up and stare at me in fear, certain that I was about to bust a cap on him. A few months later, someone did just that, snuffed him in his bed.

I also remember the time that a woman was raped in the alley during the wee hours of the morning. Echoes of Kitty

Genovese, the attack went on for a good hour or more, the residents of the two buildings ignoring the woman's pleas for help.

When it was all over, she had some choice words. You all some rotten motherfuckers, she said.

The next day people justified their indifference: She ain't got no better sense than to be out in a dark alley at that time of night.

Yeah. Looking for trouble.

Did you see the way she was dressed?

A goddamn shame.

She got to be a prostitute.

Serves her right.

But episodes like these were rare in the alley. The men did their thing on weekends and holidays, and the rest of the time the alley was the gaming space for us young folk, a place where we played baseball and softball, and "off the wall" with either a rubber ball or tennis ball. We also played basketball, although we had neither hoop nor net. Improvising, we would shoot the rock over a slanted telephone wire.

Tomboy Bernadette, aka Bonnie, was the best basketball player in the neighborhood, our Dr. J. She had all the moves and never lost a game of one-on-one. But Bonnie was also the toughest kid in the neighborhood regardless of gender. She could throw hands. For some reason she always butted heads with Little Man, a wannabe thug from a thug family who lived in the adjacent building. Bonnie always made quick work of him. And he was not the forgiving sort. After one ass-kicking he hurried home only to return to the alley a short while later with a rusty sword. Bonnie disarmed him then kicked his ass again.

Bonnie was also my first girlfriend. We became an item when I was eight years old; she was a year older. One day we went down into the basement of our building to kiss, chaste kisses on the lips, no tongue, childish activity. This went on until she asked me, Do you want to kiss with our clothes off? Scared, I found some reason to decline her offer.

By the time we were teenagers, it was clear to everyone in our circle that Bonnie was gay, or bisexual, although I don't believe that she ever openly admitted it. For a time she played basketball for a professional league, then after the league failed she decided to go to college. She taught in the public schools for a few years before doing graduate work in secondary education that landed her a well-paying job as a high school principal.

Although Bonnie was fearless in many ways, she never flaunted her sexuality in the manner that my good friend Lamont would. Lamont was the first openly gay person that I knew. From the age of ten he acted like a girl and caught hell for it. Even his mother called him a "bitch." (Bitch, didn't I tell you to wash the dishes? ... Bitch, didn't I tell you to take out the garbage? ... Bitch, didn't I tell you to wash the laundry?)

But Lamont felt no affinity for Bonnie. One day when we were hanging out—we were both about sixteen, our birthdays only days apart—he started badmouthing her. I saw her having sex right there in the bushes with Donald and Alfonso, he said. They were taking turns with her. Lamont scrunched up his face. It was disgusting. I almost threw up.

Lamont also claimed that he had slept with all of my male friends. He had many claims.

Lamont was among an assortment of outcasts who hung

out in the alley. But Don is the person who stands out most in my memory, a slow-moving obese mentally retarded man who was at least a decade older than I was and who lived in the adjacent building with his parents and three brothers. A borderline funny uncle, Don was always anxious to talk to you about sex and to show you the sexual paraphernalia he kept on his person, such as a deck of playing cards that featured photos of women with three "titties."

In comparison to him, Don's brothers all seemed to be pretty strait-laced, with the exception of Rod, a bespectacled soft spoken guy who some people thought was weak, a mamma's boy, a closet sissy. One time, some dude got into an argument with Rod, cursed him out thoroughly and called him one vile name after another. Pushing the issue, he undid his zipper, pulled out his dick and pissed all over Rod's pants legs. The dude started laughing. I just pissed on you, nigger. What you gon do about it?

Rod disappeared into the apartment building where he lived and after a time came back with his father's pistol. He aimed the pistol and shot the dude in the chest.

That family's misfortune continued. In the eighties, the third oldest brother Michael succumbed to AIDS, having supposedly contracted the virus from prostitutes who worked Johns at the Zanzibar Motel up on Stoney Island. It was a blow.

Michael and some of the young bloods of his generation in the neighborhood liked to keep company with a gay man named Greg, and they were quite accepting of him. Greg was a tall handsome man fond of showing off his long legs in hot pants. He fell victim to AIDS just months before Michael.

I feared for Lamont. He did not fare well in high school,

each day having to battle some forrealassnigger who sought to give this fag a beat down. Then AIDS started doing the beating, striking down fags all across America. One afternoon in the early eighties found Lamont sitting across from me at our kitchen table. A few years earlier, my mom and I had moved to a larger apartment across the hall in the 1826 entrance to our courtyard building. But the move was little comfort, for I was hell-bent on leaving that building, longed to be elsewhere at a time when AIDS and crack cocaine set the world I knew on fire.

Sitting there at the table, I had only one question for Lamont. Aren't you worried about AIDS?

No, Lamont said. I don't sleep with too many guys.

Lamont succumbed to AIDS in 1987, around the time that I left 1826 East 72nd Street for a pricey studio apartment on the Northside in Wrigleyville. Wrigleyville was a pleasant place to live, a quiet and safe space of neighborly and open-minded people, a world apart from South Shore. I had few complaints. The one thing, it was not far enough away from the myriad personal and social complexities that I was trying to escape. So all I could do was await the day when I would do just that, by hook or crook, the day when I would construct a vessel and set sail on Lake Michigan—sail until I reached home.

when the moon fit
in my window

ALICE EVE COHEN

hen I visited my childhood home on Google
Earth, my first thought was that nothing had
changed. Our little house on the corner was still
gray and white—white on the first floor, gray on the second
floor, white shutters, shaded by the same maple tree I used to
climb. Green hedges still lined the small, sloping front yard. I
grew up in that house, from the age of three, in 1957, until the
summer before I left for college, in 1972.

Of course, plenty has changed in forty-three years. A quick
Google search revealed that the modest house my parents
bought in 1957 for $19,000 is now appraised at $500,000. The
shiny new sedan in the driveway bears no resemblance to our
1960s Rambler station wagon (think fake wood paneling), nor to
our first family car—a curvaceous, turquoise Dodge sedan (think
no seatbelts, no air-conditioning, broken heater). When we
drove home from visits to Grandpa in Brooklyn or Nana Leah
in Far Rockaway on freezing winter nights, my sisters and I

shivered in the icy cold back seat, huddled together under a plaid wool blanket. If we were asleep when we got home, my daddy lifted us in his muscular arms and carried us inside, sheltered on his warm chest.

In what was once my second floor bedroom window, there is now an air conditioner, rendering the window permanently shut. A shame. I remember how on summer nights, I kept the window wide open. From my bed, I'd gaze at the full moon, marveling that it was small enough to fit within the window frame, small enough for me to cover with the palm of my hand. I relished the warm breeze that made my translucent curtain flutter and billow. I loved lying in bed, listening to summer's symphony of night sounds: crickets and other night creatures, the yowl of tomcats and flirtatious meowing of girl-cats in heat; the distant train with its Doppler crescendo and decrescendo as it rolled down the tracks. And every night of my childhood, I listened to my dad playing downstairs on the grand piano in the living room. Chopin, Beethoven, Gershwin, Mozart, and Debussy were my lullabies. Most nights at bedtime, Mom stroked my back and recited in her magical singsong, "X marks the spot, with a dot, dot, dot, and a dash and a line, and a big question mark. Trickle up, trickle down, trickle all around. With a pinch a squeeze and a cool ocean breeze."

Google Earth's street view reveals that the maple tree in the front yard is now twice as tall as it was when I was a kid. I would jump as high as I could to grab the lowest branch, wrap my legs around it, hoist myself up, and climb into the higher branches —an ideal location for spying, a favorite hobby of mine. My gray cat, Amanda, often accompanied me (though when she was a kitten, she climbed so high she was scared to come down and we had to call the fire department to rescue her). My sisters Madeline and Jennifer weren't tree-climbers, so I thought of it as *my* tree. I loved that tree. Sometimes in the dark, I hugged the trunk. I liked the way the bark smelled, especially after it rained. In Google Earth's street view, you can't see the treetop, but the lowest branch must be fifteen feet high. No good for climbing, unless you're a cat.

Most striking difference, *Then* vs. *Now*: in the street view of the neighborhood (dated August 2013) there's not a human in sight, even on a dappled and sunny summer day. Not even when I navigate up and down several blocks. There are plenty of cars parked in driveways, so some folks must have been at home when this image was captured, but there's not a soul outdoors. Empty sidewalks, empty yards. It's Twilight Zone-esque. When I was growing up, there were children playing outside at all hours, especially in summer. Unsupervised boys and girls skipping down the sidewalk, running through each other's yards. Bicycling, skateboarding, racing, playing tag, jumping rope, siblings pushing each other on squeaky swing sets. On warm summer evenings, a dozen or more kids, ranging from toddlers to teens, gathered for spontaneous backyard games of kickball, badminton, spud, freeze-tag, hide-and-seek. While fireflies blinked on and off at dusk, we chanted street songs and rhymes, to decide who was "it" ("*Eeny meeny miny mo, catch a tiger by the toe, if he hollers let him go, my mother says to pick this very best one, and you are it,*"), or choose teams ("*Engine, engine, number nine, Going down Chicago line, If the train goes off the track, Do you want your money back?*"), or to retrieve the last one hiding ("*Olly olly um free! Come out, come out, wherever you are!*"). Other chants and songs were meant to tease. (*"Nya nya nya nya nya"* and *"Alice and Harry sitting in a tree, K-I-S-S-I-N-G, first comes love, then comes marriage, then comes baby in the baby carriage."*) Our games lasted till it was dark, or until our moms called us in to dinner, whichever came first.

In the present-day image of the neighborhood, where is everyone? Where are the kids? Maybe 21st Century family values preclude children going outside to play unsupervised. Are they all inside behind closed windows, in their air-conditioned rooms? Are they staring at computer screens, instead of playing outdoors... Like I am now? Like my daughters are? Yeesh. I guess so.

I grew up in Mamaroneck, a suburb of New York City in Westchester county. There were high-income sections of town (near Long Island Sound and the beach), and a low-income section of town (behind the train tracks). In-between were middle class areas, such as the modest, blue-collar neighborhood where my family lived. In the fifties and sixties, most of the moms were, well... moms. Moms and housewives. The fathers all worked. The dad diagonally across from us was a policeman. The dad across the street made a living by selling hotdogs and sodas from his truck, illustrated with a giant hand-painted hotdog, which he parked near the entrance to the New England Throughway.

My parents didn't fit in. My mother was a sociologist and an adjunct professor of sociology at Columbia University, Pace, and City College, always trying to complete her Ph.D. dissertation, which proved an elusive goal. She was a feminist, ahead of her time. But being *of* her time—pre-Women's Movement—

meant that in addition to working she was also a full-time mom and housewife. When I was a little girl, my father was a piano teacher; later, when he realized he couldn't support a family by teaching piano, he started his own business.

Our neighbors were Italian Catholic and Irish Catholic. In December, every house, except ours, was decorated with Christmas lights. We were the only Jews in the neighborhood. This was a problem. My dad loved to sail, but he was excluded from the yacht club because he was Jewish. The children next door enthusiastically told us why they were wearing their Sunday best: "Today is the day the Jews killed Christ!" Anti-Semitism came in waves, sometimes subtle and unspoken, sometimes harsh and explicit. In the Google Earth image, the driveway pavement is now black. When I lived there, our driveway was pale concrete. One morning, we woke up to find the word J-E-W painted across our driveway in enormous black letters, and all of our bicycle tires slashed.

My neighborhood often felt to me like a hostile environment, but my house never did. Home was safe. I loved my family—my baby sister Jennifer, my big sister Madeline, Mommy and Daddy. I loved our pets: Amanda the cat and her many litters of kittens, our hamster, mouse, turtles, goldfish, the occasional toad I caught and kept in a box in the backyard, the abandoned baby birds I rescued and fed with mashed bread and milk from a eyedropper till they were strong enough to fly away. I loved my artwork, my books and stuffed animals, my clarinet and recorder. I loved playing duets with Dad, all of us singing folksongs around the piano. I loved that our house was filled with music and dancing and singing, and the yummy smells of Mom's cooking and baking. I loved my room—it had one wall painted red, on which Mom allowed me and my girl-friends to write and draw anything we wanted. Our house was tiny and cozy, with a fireplace in the living room where we toasted marshmallows in winter, and a backyard for hide-and-seek and snowball fights.

As a child, I felt deeply loved. In adolescence, things got terribly complicated for me. My relationship with my mother became stormy and angry and troubled. But when I was a kid, home was warm and safe.

My immediate neighborhood was a different story. Beside the threatening current of anti-Semitism, there were no girls my age, just a gaggle of boys in my grade. The boy across the street chased me home from school and attacked me on a regular basis, kicking me, pushing me in the mud, and throwing rocks at me. (I belatedly confronted him, when I was forty years old and bumped into him while on vacation at a national park. He said, "I don't remember doing those terrible things to you, but I'm sure you're right. My mother told me I was a really mean kid." He apologized.)

When I was in kindergarten, Harry, a very sweet boy in my neighborhood and my class, asked me to marry him. I said yes. "Guess what! Harry and I are going to get married!" I announced at dinner that night. My big sister Madeline laughed at me and said, "You think you will, but you won't." (I was enraged, but of course Madeline was right.) At my tenth high school reunion, I discovered that Harry had in fact proposed to at least three girls in kindergarten. Even as grown women, we all felt jealous, annoyed that we'd been cheated on as five-year-olds. But at Daniel Warren Elementary School in 1959, I was crazy about my fiancé. It's fun, today on Google Earth, to be electronically reminded of the thrill of walking to his house for lunch after half-day kindergarten. Harry's dad was an extroverted and whimsical guy. One night, the dad stopped by our house with his little pet monkey on his shoulder. We were celebrating Hanukah, the candles were burning in the menorah, my dad was playing "Hava Nagila" on the piano, and my sisters and I danced and spun around till we were dizzy. The monkey got into the act, chasing us, scampering and jumping and circling our living room, mischievously screeching and squealing, jumping on us, pulling our hair, and finally—to our immense amusement—pooping on the wooden floor. My sisters and I laughed till we cried. It was a great night.

When I was seventeen, two weeks before I started college, my parents sold the old house and bought a ranch house on the more affluent side of town, near the beach. I was just about to leave home, so the new house never felt like home to me. I was only there on school breaks. The little house I grew up in is the house I dream of.

I have a recurrent dream—that dream, which I understand is ubiquitous among space-challenged New York City apartment dwellers, where you open a door and find the extra room you forgot was there. In *my* dream, the room I discover is usually my childhood bedroom. The window is wide open, framing the full moon, and I hear night sounds of crickets, the distant train, and a Beethoven piano sonata wafting up from downstairs.

my dingbat

POROCHISTA KHAKPOUR

One: Tropical Gardens

Here is 1675 *Amberwood Drive, South Pasadena, California, 91030,* the apartment complex I grew up in. The first apartment, my home from 1st grade to 11th, was #31, a third floor unit on the northwest end of the building, two bedrooms and one bathroom for the four of us. Then, my senior year of high school, we moved into #19, which was in the southeast end, two stories, finally with two bed-rooms and two bathrooms. Up until the age of 17, I shared a room with my brother, but my final year of high school I got to have the first room of my own since I was an infant.

The complex is all cream—perhaps simply off-white with time—with dark green trimmings, the words *Tropical Gardens* dashed off in the sort of cursive you might find on the cover of a '50s homemaking magazine or perhaps adorning a cake. Built in 1957, it wasn't even thirty years old when we moved in in 1984. Because of the parking garage underneath, all the units had these overhanging balconies, which felt so luxurious to me—

my favorite feature of my home, especially since we had no yard. But it also felt like the building was on stilts. I remember worrying about whether it could handle a big earthquake, even though I went through two big ones there—the most powerful I'd ever experienced, the Northridge Quake of 1994, on the day of my sixteenth birthday. There was no real damage to our building, which shocked me.

The carpet in the first apartment was a light brown, the color of coffee with milk, made of a terrible matted thin fur, like the coat of my poodle but not nearly as attractive. The second was thicker, shaggier, a swirl of dark brown, beige, and white, like a commercial for all three chocolate shades in one or the melted remains of a chocolate sundae. The ceilings were low and plain, but there were ample windows—the first apartment had a view of the railroad and the War Memorial Building and that one mansion I was obsessed with on the other side of the tracks that I made up countless stories about; the second apartment faced out onto Amberwood Drive, a quiet street, only disturbed occasionally by a passing car, a dog walker, a skater, a leaf blower.

These apartments are the only homes of my upbringing, since I don't remember that first apartment in Tehran, the temporary homes along the way, or that first American apartment in Alhambra, also small and dingy certainly, also brown and beige probably, and also nothing to boast about.

We came to South Pasadena for the schools, a very solid public school system, everyone always said and continues to say (I just went to a party of New Yorkers who had recently relocated there and everyone said the same thing: "You move here for your kids, for the schools"). All the walls of the living room were covered in books, shelf upon shelf, mostly yellow spines of the *National Geographics* my father had tried so hard to collect as he continued to subscribe. Also, many sets of second-hand encyclopedias, as he could never afford a new set for us. Framed illustrations of old Persian Empire relics, photos of us, vases, bad couches. At one point in the midst of all that brown, my parents bought a red, white, and blue plaid couch—they claimed they loved it, but I knew it was considerably marked down on sale. It was one of the hardest visuals I had to endure in my youth.

I guess it doesn't surprise me that now, five years since I've set foot in the building (my parents finally convinced themselves a few years ago that they'd never return to Iran—after three decades, renting no longer made sense—and they bought a condo in nearby cheaper Glendale, where I visit now, where, in fact, I am writing this), it takes this project to teach me the name of *what* I lived in. I traditionally would describe it as "the kitschy '60s apartment district in the part of South Pasadena all the rich kids called the South Pasadena projects," because to live in South Pasadena meant you lived in a home, a Craftsman, a Victorian, anything, but definitely not an apartment. It also does not surprise me that the name is as absurd, ugly, mean, and wonderfully wacky as it should be . . .

Two: Dingbats

1998: Vivian, Natasha Lyonne's teenage character in *The Slums of Beverly Hills*, knows its name. "*Casa Bella,* another dingbat—that's what they're called. *Dingbats.* Two-story apartment buildings featuring cheap rents and fancy names. They promise the good life but never deliver."

1999: *LA Weekly*, Mark Frauenfelder wrote a column called "How I Came To Love The Dingbat": "You couldn't make an uglier building if you tried. Los Angeles is full of dingbats— boxy two-story apartments supported by stilts, with open stalls below for parking. (Their name is likely to have been coined by architect Francis Ventre while he was lecturing at UCLA in the early '70s.) Thousands of the inexpensive 16-unit structures were built in the late '50s and early '60s to accommodate the huge number of people moving to Southern California. Forty years later, the smog-stained, sagging dingbats are still here, and have become as much a part of the LA landscape as medfly traps and on-ramp pistachio vendors. Recently, my interest in dingbats swelled even more after becoming exposed to the contagious enthusiasm of Lesley M. Siegel, an LA artist who has photographed over 2,000 of the signs that are sometimes attached to the outside of dingbats. With names like *The Belvan, The Hayworth House, The Riviera Palms, The South Pacific, The Unique,* and *The UnXled,* these painted, jigsaw-cut wood signs have been a source of fascination for Siegel even before she started photographing them in 1990. Spelled out in loopy script or whimsical lettering, the names provide look-alike dingbats with a sense of individuality. More importantly, like incense, they mask the acrid tang of life in an oversized shoebox with an air of relaxed, tropical, exotic, or well-heeled splendor."

If you comb through the Internet you will find a shocking amount of "in praise of the dingbat" articles, particularly from the '90s.

Three: The Raymond

The South Pasadena Projects wasn't all dingbats, or at least it didn't start out that way. Pasadena was settled by Midwesterners who wanted to have temperate winters in the Wild West, mainly the ailing, the elderly, the rich. And South Pasadena was a big draw: my dingbat and all the adjacent dingbats were once all the site of a major hotel that attracted dignitaries and luminaries from all over the state, if not the country. Raymond Hill, as the neighborhood is known now, was once Bacon Hill and comprised only *The Raymond*. It took three years and more than 250 workers to build: 55 acres of South Pasadena's Bacon Hill that was blasted and flattened for this four-story Second-Empire-style building with two hundred guest rooms, forty-three bathrooms, forty water closets, and a 104-foot tall tower. It finally opened its doors on November 17, 1886, with an inaugural ball of 1,500 guests, that *The Los Angeles Times* called "perhaps the most extensive social affair in the history of the county."

It was Southern California's leading resort hotel until Easter Sunday 1895, when one of the Raymond's eighty chimneys landed on the hotel's wood roof and burned the structure down. It took six years for Walter Raymond to rebuild and reopen *The Raymond*, this time with double the rooms and more amenities. It took the Great Depression to down the hotel the second and final time—it was foreclosed in 1931 and was demolished in 1934. After a few attempts at various housing developments the '50s brought the neighborhood to its recent incarnation: dingbat life.

Four: Raymond Hill

These days I think *so much happened there*, while when I lived
there it seemed nothing happened at all. I can see myself at
seven, hunched over the white Kmart desk, with the Disney
curtains always drawn above me, and a pile of books I could
barely read at my side—paperback Shakespeare, second-hand
guides to literature, dictionary, thesaurus—a red pen with ink
that smelled like strawberries in my hand, scrawling in careful
cursive what would be novel after novel, practice for a future I
had imagined for myself in this faraway land named New York
City, where I knew writers lived. I see myself crying into a
jeweled compact my mother had given me, horrified by the ugli-
ness of my reflection, especially when faced with my mother,
the great beauty. I see my father's violent fits. I see the constant
shame of sharing a room with a brother five years younger
when you are already into your teens. I see the Casio, the
Walkman, the record player, the mixtapes, the boom box, what
little escape contemporary music could provide. I think of the
droughts, the El Niño rains, the earthquakes, and those '80s
serial killers never too far away. I think of my first American
natural disaster (I'd already been through the unnatural ones,
war, in Iran), the great fire of October 1984, right outside my
bedroom window, Ole's Hardware Store, that killed a handful
of people; for years we thought it *was* somewhat natural, an
electrical issue compounded by October heat, but it turned out
to be the work of a serial arsonist who was also a prominent fire
investigator, who was linked to the crime ten years later when
federal prosecutors found he'd written novels that were con-

fessions of sorts, that detailed his hand in several major fires of the '80s. I think of walking to and from school—like eating cafeteria food instead of a lovingly packed lunch, it was a subject of shame for us South Pasadena Project kids—and so much crying in the bedroom, in the bathroom, and perhaps most of all on that balcony, a thing that even in a dingbat felt glorious indeed, even as it precariously hovered in a sort of heaven—a smog filled one; I remember the constant haze and smog of my youth, the sky always as beige as those terrible carpets—reminding me then, as it does now, that I can be entirely of a place and yet in another place entirely.

4 3 0 5   n i a g a r a

L A U R A   M I L L E R

D id I not know we were moving that day, or did I just not understand what it meant to move? I was nine, and I'd never moved house before. I came home from school one afternoon and our house was empty, shockingly so, the kitchen cupboard doors swinging loose as slatterns, exposing empty shelves. It was home, the only one I'd ever known, but it was suddenly alien and bereft. There was really no point in being there anymore, yet where else would I go?

My parents had deputized one of their friends, a stranger to me, to wait for me there and I remember her sipping a glass of wine, although God only knows if that's true. Wine-sipping was the quintessential annoying adult mannerism in my mind. I hated her. I could not believe I would never be in that place again, that I had somehow missed this crucial fact in the excitement over the prospect of finally getting my own room.

That house is gone, so transformed by subsequent owners that the only way I could identify it the last time I visited San Diego was by peering at the street numbers. The monuments of our childhood—those bay windows, that backyard fence, the family dog—seem as eternal as the earth and sky until suddenly they disappear. When you're a child, you have no idea which of the world's fixtures are vulnerable to such vanishings.

But this is about the house we left that house for, and the lanky tree that stood in front of it on a rectangular slice of grass between the sidewalk and the street. I can't tell you what variety of tree it was, only that it had pale, scarred bark, and that the spot where someone had cut off an undesirable branch, long before we lived there, was marked by a knot that resembled a human eye. You can see it in countless family photos, where we all stood squinting into the Southern California light, due to my mother's unshakeable conviction that a snapshot-taker should always stand with her back to the sun.

I lived there for the next nine years, until I went off to college, and then came back for no more than a few days at a time. I didn't miss it. But that hasn't kept me from saving, like a prize, the screenshot I took of its Google Street View image in 2013. Google's shot has the tree, and the little red MG convertible my brother parked underneath it during one of those periods when, his finances in temporary disarray, he moved back into that four-bedroom ranch house with my mother. I'm sure he thought that the tree, like the house, would always be there, too.

By the time I captured that image from Google, though, the tree was gone and so was the car, because one day the tree fell on it. The house was still there—I was sitting in it—but my mother wasn't. Over the course of nine months in 2012, she fell apart, beginning with her mind and then progressing to everything else. I'd visited her in February, when she seemed occasionally checked-out, but I'd blamed that on her poorly maintained hearing aids. By August, she needed all-day care, and at the end of September, she died of a stroke. She was seventy-seven.

The following summer, when my siblings and I gathered to clean out the house, only Google still lived in a world where the tree, the car and my mother persisted. The team that photographed the cross street even caught my brother taking something out of the MG's trunk, although they didn't get my mother. Still, her car is in the driveway, and when I look at that picture, I know she's in there somewhere.

It was because of the house that I didn't see my mother during her final illness. We planned to fix it up and rent it out to help pay for her care, as we expected her to need it for several more years. My two sisters and I agreed that I'd reserve my vacation time to manage that project, since they were handling, respectively, her complicated financial and medical affairs. I'd fly across country, supervise whatever needed to be done to make the place acceptable to tenants, and then, later in the year, visit her in Arizona for the holidays. Then, abruptly, she was gone. I hadn't realized she could do that, or maybe I just couldn't imagine how vacant the world would seem afterwards.

When we were finally able to sell the place almost a year later, everything had changed, except on Google Street View. In that world—assembled with a strangely pleasing documentary detachment so different from the aspirational strain of our family photos—the tree, the MG, my brother, my mother's Toyota, survived, just another snippet of mundane suburban life, preserved in passing by strangers.

This time, however, I knew it wouldn't last. Digital media offer the illusion that the information we stash on it can be easily archived forever, but the media themselves, as well as the formats of our files, are always furiously changing. The new is all that matters to it. By the time you want that old stuff again, if you want it again, you better hope that it isn't stored on a floppy disk or in an obsolete word processing program.

I'm not sure when it happened, but it wasn't so long after we'd cleared the house of my mother's Hummel figurines, the countless greeting cards she'd saved since the 1960s, her beloved Le Creuset cookware, and the clothes, smelling dustily of her. I checked Google Street View again a few months later and the front of the house had been transformed, the little porch she'd installed razed, and the old-fashioned, mid-century decorative stonework erased, replaced by a simple portico.

I told my siblings that I liked to think of a new family living there, filling those rooms, which had become so quiet in the past thirty years while my mother waited for one of her feckless sons to hit another rough patch and request a few months of refuge. That's true; it's a house, not a memorial, and life, like the bacterial evolution of technologies, can only go in one direction. But I'm glad I saved those screenshots, for however long they last.

smalltown
canadian girl

JUSTINE MUSK

One

I read somewhere that a person has two homes: the place where you were born (literally, not metaphorically), and the place that fits your soul. If you are lucky, they are one and the same.

My son wants to know when I will take him to Canada and show him my hometown, but I'm not sure I will ever go back. We look up my parents' house on Google Maps from where we sit at the kitchen table. The breeze sweeps in through the open glass doors, carrying scents of eucalyptus. Together my son and I walk the little Google dude along the streets I walked a lifetime ago, when I could not seriously believe that I would ever reach the age I am now. What I did believe in—with such intensity that I could practically run my fingers along the edges of my future—was that the rest of my life, my *real* life, would happen Somewhere Else. I would journey to a strange and mythical land, otherwise known as Los Angeles.

"The streets look so... " My son tilts his blond head. "... so country," he finally says. "So wide and clean and empty."

My son's childhood is unfolding rather differently than mine.

"Your father is worried that your kids are not connected to reality," my mother told me once. We were standing outside the front door of the house in Bel Air, after my divorce and before the move to Brentwood. My ex had taken the kids to St. Barts for the holidays and we were awaiting their return.

I could feel myself get huffy.

I said, "My kids are connected to reality!"

The gates swung open and a long black limousine rolled carefully up the steep driveway. The driver stepped out to open the passenger door, revealing my sleepy tousled children. "Here they are," the driver announced. They were over an hour late. My ex had his own jet and his own sense of time. Punctuality didn't happen until he got there. He brought it with him. He was never late; you were early and just didn't know it.

I could feel my mother looking at me.

"Okay," I muttered. "They're connected to *a* reality. It's just maybe not, you know, *the* reality."

Two

A boyfriend once gave me a t-shirt with SMALLTOWN GIRL on the front. We were sitting in a bistro in Santa Monica with a few of my friends, who had all grown up in big cities. They knew little about my life before California. They cocked a collective eyebrow at the shirt.

"Because she is," my boyfriend said.

He considered it something that we had in common, although his hometown was four times the size of mine. Also, he had been one of the popular kids. When news got out about his divorce, women approached his father in the streets and asked him to pass on their phone numbers.

I was joking without joking. "Does this ... " making a dramatic gesture along the length of my body ... "look *smalltown* to you?"

He said, "What does that even *mean?*"

Throughout the rest of our (doomed) relationship, he would say *smalltown girl*, and I would lob my napkin at his face.

He said, "You don't like it when I call you that."

Three

The backyard of my childhood home bordered a wetland that froze in winter and turned swampy in spring. Nothing prevented its residents—or pilgrims passing through—from crossing our property line. Ducks waddled up between the trees, looking for the corn my father scattered every morning. He reported his sightings: a coyote, a deer, once a mink. A raccoon that stole the cheese from a live trap set just for him. A skunk that my father caught instead.

"Damn crows," my father grumbled, moving his pipe to the other side of his mouth, "They scare off the birds, hog the feeder. I could shoot those bastards."

As if this was a place where you sat in your yard with a shotgun on your lap.

No.

You were polite.

You were Canadian.

My cousin went out on the lake with my dad. My cousin was eight. As they drew along shore, he saw a frog sunning on a rock, and smashed it with his paddle. My father pulled over the canoe—or whatever it is that you do with canoes—and yelled in his face for a solid half hour.

"It made an impression," my cousin says now. "I never again smashed an amphibian. I respect and honor the amphibians."

Four

My father told me firmly and unequivocally that he did not see us ever getting a dog. Ever.

The next morning he mentioned a young silky terrier.

"We're just going to look at him," he warned me in the car, "so don't get your hopes up. We will not be taking him home. Under no conditions whatsoever."

We named him Jake.

I took him for walks that grew long and meandering. I unclipped him on the greenbelt, moved through patterns of sunlight and shadow, breathed in pine. I daydreamed my life into being: *I write books and have affairs and travel to other countries and speak foreign languages. I drive a black Porsche 911 like Lucas Davenport in John Sandford's series of thrillers. I live in a house with a koi pond in back, like Alex Delaware in Jonathan Kellerman's series of thrillers. I wear an Armani pantsuit with the jacket buttoned over nothing, and exchange knowing looks with intriguing men. I grow my hair long.*

When my sister and I discovered Nancy Friday's ground-breaking books describing women's sexual fantasies, we compared notes and confided our own. I got so wrapped up in plot and character, went into such a depth of backstory, that my sister nagged me to get to the sex part.

Five

I read novels by American authors about American kids. They were always snacking on Ding-Dongs. What, I asked my mother, is a Ding-Dong?

She wasn't sure.

As she browsed the aisles at Blockbuster Video, I gravitated to the dangerous covers. I was scared of them but liked the forbidden-apple thrill.

"Mom," I said, trailing her out onto the sidewalk. "What does 'castrated' mean?"

"What?"

I had read the synopsis of a movie called *I Spit On Your Grave*, about a woman who takes inventive revenge on each of her multiple assailants.

My mother said, hurriedly, "Something ... to do with the spine."

During long car rides, I would ask my parents from the back seat:

"What does 'erection' mean?"

"What is a 'wet dream'?"

"What is 'men-stroo-ation'?"

I had discovered Judy Blume.

Six

Sometimes on American television, an actor or comedian would start talking in a strange way and add 'eh?' after every sentence. I realized that they were imitating—or thought they were imitating—Canadian accents.

The 'eh' aspect of the stereotype eluded me. (It bemused me that a Canadian stereotype existed.) When I read Margaret Atwood novels, or watched episodes of *Degrassi Junior High*, I noted how the characters were not running around saying, 'eh'? I didn't see this in real life either.

Although we did seem drawn to sweaters with images of moose on them.

Sometimes geese.

Seven

My father lamented Canada's choice of national animal. "America has the bald eagle!" he pointed out. "Russia has the bear! And Canada has..."—he would pause for dramatic effect —"...the mighty beaver!"

I knew this already.

"What message does that send to the world? How could that *ever* strike terror in the hearts of our enemies?"

"Canada doesn't have enemies," I told him. "We apologize too much."

"Hypothetically speaking."

"The beaver is very industrious. Also semi-aquatic."

"It's a *rodent*. It gnaws through *tree trunks*."

Eight

A magazine asked its readers to finish this sentence: "As Canadian as ... "

They were looking for the Canadian equivalent of "As American as apple pie." They had noticed that there didn't seem to be any. The best answer would win a cash prize.

Nine

I fantasized about Luke Skywalker—not the whiny farm kid, but the tormented Jedi in black who could move things with his mind. I was his sleek, gifted protégée, and we'd engage in well-choreographed training scenes that sizzled with sexual tension.

I developed a crush on Kurt Browning, the first figure skater to land a quadruple jump in competition. We, his countrymen and -women, adored him wildly and wanted him to win Olympic gold. When he fell in the short program, I felt sad for him, for me, for the nation. Then I went to step class.

He was gracious in his interviews. Today we would consider him *authentic*. Back then I considered him a hunky blue-eyed love object with unusually intricate footwork.

Kurt's figure-skating nemesis—domestic, not international —was Elvis Stojko, a gifted jumper who said to hell with the rules! He would be his own man!

He skated to techno.

After losing the gold, again, to Kurt, Stojko told the interviewer that he was a loner. He was like—he put his hands together and glided them through the air—a bird of prey, soaring high in the sky on his own brand of wind. The interviewer cocked her head at him.

Note how he said: *bird of prey.*

He did not say: *industrious semi-aquatic rodent who gnaws down trees for a living.*

Ten

One of the creatures passing through our backyard was a tall skinny bad boy named Warwick. I knew him from university. He liked to dance. Despite his family's wealth—or because of it —he wore out his possessions until they fell apart. His wallet. His cowboy boots. He patched them back together with duct tape.

One night a group of us were talking in the kitchen of his parents' Toronto penthouse. His parents were away at the time. I made a dramatic hand gesture to underscore a point I was making, or trying to make, and dropped my glass of bourbon. It shattered all across the gleaming marble. Warwick made eye contact with me. He opened his hand and let drop his own glass. It fell like a bomb and broke just as fiercely.

Everybody laughed, including the aspiring writer who wrote down his impression of me from that night: *Justine seems lonely, like she doesn't have many friends.*

Warwick arrived on his motorcycle one summer afternoon to take me away to the penthouse. His parents were away at the time. I chose to not mention that to my own. That afternoon he lounged alongside my father in a matching lawn chair while my mother brought out roast beef sandwiches layered with slabs of cheddar. Warwick marveled over the sandwiches, and the fact that she had made them herself.

My mother took me aside and said, "Don't you get the feeling that he had a lonely childhood?"

Loneliness, I learned, is like rain. It falls everywhere.

Eleven

When the drama club staged an adaptation of *The Sting*, I hassled the director—also my English teacher—to make the Paul Newman character a woman. I wanted that part and knew I could do it. He cast me as a reformed dance hall queen (not in the movie) who narrates the story to a journalist over tea.

"I know you lead a controlled lifestyle," the director told me, "but you have a certain sensuality about you." This was news to me, and interesting.

I spent the entire play sitting at a table in the corner of the stage, sometimes in the spotlight but mostly in the dark, shifting for comfort, crossing and uncrossing my legs. In the final scene I had to saunter down the stage, give the audience a wink, and strut away as the curtain dropped. The director mentioned my pigeon toed stance, and we looked down at my feet in white sneakers.

"You have the body language of a sixteen year old girl," he chastised me.

My voice reminded him of Lauren Bacall. I tried to watch *The Big Sleep* but lost interest halfway through. The director told me in front of cast and crew to undo another button on my blouse.

A girl from a good Christian family told me, "You look like such a slut!"

"You ain't seen nothing yet," I said, lying back on the table and kicking my legs up.

Everybody laughed.

Twelve

I liked the story behind Lauren Bacall's signature style of delivering her lines with her chin slightly tucked, her eyes looking up at the camera. The director told her to keep doing it. It was sultry and coy.

But she wasn't sultry, she said. She was just nervous.

Thirteen

My younger sister went to work at Blockbuster Video. She told me how two of her male colleagues hated me because they thought I was a bitch. I didn't think I had exchanged words with either of them. I had no idea who they were.

I started to feel hurt. Then it occurred to me not to care. It was a strange and revolutionary thought.

"She was in here the other night," one boy told my sister as she prepared to start her shift. "She was walking around the store. Flipping her hair around."

It was true. My hair was very long and fell into my face.

"She thinks she's so hot," the boy said.

"Maybe it's because," my sister said, "she is."

Fourteen

There was a girl a couple of grades below me who lived in The Townhouses. That was what we called the low-income housing along a major hillside street.

In junior high, she bloomed.

I would see her navigating the sidewalk in the rain, holding her umbrella, wearing a stylish fitted minidress. Boys my own age rarely talked to me. But I knew they talked to her.

When I was about to leave for university on partial scholarship, I stopped by a fast food kiosk in the mall. I recognized her immediately. She was still extremely pretty. She turned from the cash register, which is when I saw that she was nearing the end of her pregnancy.

Fifteen

My sister went to work at a convenience store. One night when she was alone, she looked up from sweeping the floor and saw a masked man in the doorway.

"A *short* man," she said, "with a *huge* knife."

He was also holding a pillowcase.

She could barely speak. Or move. It was all she could do just to give him the cash.

But—she told me years later—another part of her couldn't help thinking: Your knife is that big? Really? You think there's enough cash to fill a pillowcase?

I couldn't remember how the story ended, so I texted her to ask.

She texted back: He and his buddy were bragging to all

their friends about how he robbed the Mac's Convenience Store on Hilliard Street, and a girl called the cops and turned him in.

Sixteen

The national magazine holding the "As Canadian as..." contest announced the winning entry. It went like this: "As Canadian as possible... under the circumstances."

Seventeen

I only seemed to want the boys who did not want me back. If I noticed one moving toward me, I ran in the opposite direction.

Then I fell into an infatuation with an older man who liked to quote Nietzsche and Jim Morrison.

He was saying, "There she is."

He was smiling at me, his eyes lively and warm. I chased him for months. I read *Thus Spoke Zarathustra*. When he finally started moving straight at me, I flipped my hair and held my ground.

But then I left anyway.

I met a man who told me that we were soulmates. I married him and had kids with him as if I wanted to believe him every time he said it.

I once read somewhere that the real definition of soulmate has nothing to do with being blissfully happy all of the time, hanging out with your lost and found better half, having incredible sex. Your soulmate is someone who forces your soul to grow, and growth tends to involve mess and crisis and struggle and blood. We only change when we absolutely have to: life has to crack us like an egg just to get us to do it. Maybe that's your soul-home: the place where you're forced to invent yourself.

Or maybe some people belong to certain places, and other people belong to a certain state of mind. When you are in that perspective, you are home. When you are not, you are trying to get there.

My son has announced, at age eleven, that he wants to go to UCLA so he can stay close to his family. Not for him, it seems, is that gnawing restless yearning in the bones, that hell-bent determination to get away. It has occurred to me, at age forty-three, to ask myself what it is that I've been running from all these years. Or was there something that I needed to find, and I had to come this far to find it? I don't feel at home in LA, just like I never felt at home in Peterborough, Ontario, and I am okay with that. It's that sense of not-belonging that can become, slowly and over time, its own kind of belonging. If nothing keeps me rooted, then nothing holds me back from being the woman and the writer and the mother that I need to be. I don't need to feel at home in order to be home for my son.

We close the laptop. My son pads barefoot into the kitchen and opens a drawer. I look out through the doors onto the deck, the lizard sunning itself on the redwood. My son reappears by my side holding a coffee mug filled with birdseed, and we step outside to check on the koi and feed the backyard wildlife.

where we're going

JEN MICHALSKI

"Perhaps home is not a place
but simply an irrevocable condition."
—James Baldwin, *Giovanni's Room*

When you Google "2105 E. Lamley Street" in Google Earth, the narrow, clean, completely rehabbed alley house in Baltimore City that my partner and I purchased in 2012 is not there. A vacant and boarded-up shell is in its place, one of four in the row, their brick fronts covered with a coat of taupe paint, and the doors and windows covered with long slabs of plywood. The pictures of the neighborhood were taken in 2009, during the time that the old, abandoned shells were being gutted and prepped. These pictures seem fitting, in a way. Although my partner and I have created some memories here at Lamley Street, there are not very many, certainly not as many as, say, the house we rented for five years in the county, or my childhood homes, the home I shared with my ex-girlfriend of eleven years in South Baltimore, or even my college dormitory.

The most painful lack of memories at 2105 E. Lamley Street involves my mother. She had visited the house only a handful of times, six or eight, before she died unexpectedly last October. Although most of our memories are contained within ourselves, some reside in other people, still others in places. Who does not, when stepping into her childhood home, remember the birthday when she got her first puppy or the driveway where she got her first kiss goodnight? On Lamley Street, however, I do not look at our sofa from IKEA and think of the evenings my mother read to me and my brother when we were four, or when I'd look at her magazines and didn't understand, as a seven-year-old, their appeal (although I certainly can't get enough of *Good Housekeeping* and *Vanity Fair* now). Nor do I look at our kitchen on Lamley Street, with its polished green granite counter and stainless-steel appliances, and remember the time when I was ten, waking up in my childhood home to my mother and father having a fight, going downstairs to break it up, and finding my mother on the floor, phone in her hand, calling for help, my father on top of her with a knife at her throat. I don't look at my bedroom on Lamley Street and think of the day my mother explained to me how I would get my period, or open the drawers of my dresser and inhale the scent of fresh linens she had hung on the line that day to dry.

Of course, unless we are very lucky, or very unadventurous, we rarely spend our entire lives in one place, at the very least not in the house in which we were born. In some ways, we are like hermit crabs, constantly outgrowing our shells as we graduate high school, pursue higher education in another state, find a partner, have children. But whereas hermit crabs take everything they need with them, we leave behind so many memories in those houses, those places. I often dream of every single house in which I've lived. Sometimes these dreams are like old home movies, where my mother is still young and my grandparents and other relatives are still alive. Sometimes new people are living in the houses in my dreams, but I can see the ghosts of our past still in them. Sometimes the houses are empty, and I dream I am moving back into them, trying to find a way to make them as comfortable as they were when we lived in them, sans the brown shag carpets and harvest gold stoves and linoleum floors.

The other night I dreamed of my mother in the bedroom of her house. She was holding her third Siamese cat, Sassafras Cinders, the one who passed a few years before her, and they both wore strings of those beautiful, gaudy glass necklace beads of which my mother was so fond. I complimented my mother on the color in her face, her health, how great she looked. Perhaps it *was* her, letting me know that she was okay. In this dream I visited my grandparents at their house, too. Everyone felt as if they were alive, so much so that I assumed they *were* still alive when I awoke, and it wasn't until I was outside walking our dog, Sophie, a few minutes later that it dawned on me that they were all gone, so far away, and I began to cry.

The houses remain, for now. Other people will live in them, make their own memories. Then, they will be demolished, like our boarded-up house on Google Earth, and new houses will rise from concrete and two-by-fours, with new memories still. There is no permanence in anything, and yet we build these boxes around ourselves like monuments, scrapbooks to our lives. We hide in them and sleep in them and they reflect what we think of ourselves. We fancy ourselves modernists or lovers of Jacobean future. We store the healthy food in front of the fridge and the Oreo cookies in the back. We pack memories of holidays and births and funerals in the attic, and there's a little basket we keep downstairs near the washer for all the soiled things we don't want others to see. In the end, however, time or circumstance will force us to leave these boxes also, or perhaps they will be taken away from us.

Sometimes I wish I didn't have an address, a place to be found. Like 2105 Lamley Street, if you Google "Jen Michalski," on the sidebar to the right of the search results you can find out immediately what I look like, that I live in Baltimore, that I attended St. Mary's College of Maryland, and that I have two e-mail address (one of which, ironically, is not mine). Suddenly, we have become fixed locations as well, as easily accessible as an e-mail hyperlink. It must be so freeing to be a nomad, to only have the clothes on our backs, the thoughts in our heads, the feelings in our hearts, our souls nestled safely. Not only to be homeless, but to be anonymous, with no Internet or Facebook presence to track our activities. We would never be weighed down by possessions or past. We could move, moment to moment, through the land. But it is when we die that we truly become nomadic and free. Free to live in all the houses of our past, or none at all. Free to have a home in every atom, in every second of time, of life. Free to be everything. Ironically, we will be gone entirely, findable not even by Google Earth, but our memories will remain, online, in items that have been donated to Goodwill or the Salvation Army, in the memories of others who live on, in the houses that have been resold.

I wonder whether Google Earth will ever update the picture of our house on Lamley Street, and if they do, whether we will still be living there. I wonder what sort of memories we will have created in the meantime, what love, what sadness, will embed itself in the walls and floorboards like cigarette smoke or moisture, softening foundations, warping wood. Will I publish the book that catapults me into literary stardom, and will Lamley Street become forever associated with my name the way Cathedral Street in downtown Baltimore is linked to the writer H. L. Mencken? Or will I leave this house anonymously, tasking someone else to immortalize it?

Out of curiosity, I also searched for my mother's house on Google Earth. The picture, from June 2008, is even more dated than ours, and it is only a photo of the back of the house, since my mother's house is in a private community. I zoomed in to see what was on the deck, because it was summer and I wanted to see whether my mother was growing tomatoes. What I didn't expect to see was my mother standing in the doorway to the deck. A little blurry ghost of her only, taken from a camera mounted on top of a van. But there she was, alive. I secretly hope that Google never updates the picture, that she will always live there, but I know one day I will visit the site and there will be a better pictures of her house, one of greater resolution, at closer range, and she will be long gone. And maybe by that time 2105 E. Lamley Street finally will have been built.

But where will we be, I be, ultimately? Where we were, where we are, where we will eventually wind up? Where do we find ourselves, and more importantly, where do we look?

touched by grace

Two months ago I drove past our tiny family home in Big Bend, Wisconsin on the way to the Veteran's Cemetery. My daughter Rachel was riding shotgun, my mom was in the back seat with my oldest brother, Jeff, and my dad was on Jeff's lap inside of a beautiful blue urn with a hunter and a dog painted on the outside.

I glanced at the house and slowed down to look at it for just a few seconds, stunned by how small it seemed, how unchanged, how old and, well, Big-Bend-like. In quick passing the neighborhood could have been locked inside some 1960's or '70's time warp. I could almost see myself looking out of the bedroom window and wishing I were somewhere else. Our car was filled with such sorrow, tissues flying everywhere, my beloved mother barely hanging on, that I let the thoughts of our little redbrick house and my life inside of it slip away.

This afternoon I took a virtual tour of Big Bend, which I jokingly call Large Lump when I do public speaking, and I was filled with such a flood of memories and powerful emotions that I started to cry. I was fortunate. Not only did I have fantastic, loving, fun parents, but they were smart enough to drag me out into the middle of nowhere so I could walk through the snow (barefoot, of course) two miles to St. Joseph's Catholic Grade School, run free like a wild dog through the back woods, slip through the farmer's fields across the street to steal sweet corn, and grow up four doors down from my cousins.

On my virtual tour I zoomed down Big Bend Drive, past Uncle Bob's house and across from where Mary Oakwood and the Duginski's lived and right into my surprisingly unchanged front yard. I paused right there for a long time and thought again of my father. He built the house himself, driving from Milwaukee every night after his work as a brickmason to dig the hole, build the basement, put up the walls, paint, and then worry for the next twenty-five years about how he was going to pay off Mr. King, who held our mortgage.

I am still grieving the loss of his booming laugh, quick temper, amazing spirit, lively wit, and unfailing love for me, and yet simply looking at the three-bedroom, one-bathroom house, with his big-ass flagpole still in the front yard, the flower stand by the front door he made for my mother, and the garage door that my Grandpa Bruno drove through once, made me so damn happy.

My God, we had fun in that house and in that itsy bitsy neighborhood. We had bike races on the back road where I tried to get my brothers to stop pulling dead frogs on strings behind their bikes. We built tree forts and jumped off the roof into snow banks so high they covered our windows. We helped Mr. Holtz, the farmer, bail his hay because we thought it was fun, and all he had to give us was a bottle of orange soda, something we rarely had at home. We snuck through the fields and into the woods and found a big vine and played Tarzan. We carried our ice skates across the never-busy highway and skated in the cornfields when they flooded and I pretended I was Peggy Fleming. We had all the relatives over and ate corn on the cob, and burnt food because everyone got crocked, and they let all of us cousins run wild and eat candy till we threw up behind the garage. We walked through the backyards of the houses behind us on Saturday mornings and went down to the town dump just after it closed to find cool stuff that stupid people threw away. We laughed and laughed when our friends from the city came out and they saw their first cow and it looked as if they had just been to Disneyland and run into Mickey Mouse. We thought it was thrilling when my dad fired the shotgun out the back door on special holidays. We loved it when Gloria came to babysit so my parents could go square dancing about once a year because she let us stay up late and bought us presents. We raced home every single Friday because it was the day my mom baked and we could smell bread, cookies, and pie before we ever got past the stop sign where all the kids who got to ride home in cars turned left.

We had occasional problems and people we knew died and there was always whispering about things like the bank account, and how we'd have to figure out college by ourselves, but none of that ever mattered because we were all so loved in that little house. We were loved and we learned about hard work and sacrifice and what is really important and that if we wanted something we had to find jobs. (I still wanted a new bike and not the used one, got sick of hand-me-down clothes, cried like a baby and said horrible things to my parents when I couldn't go places because we only had one car, was absolutely jealous of all my friends who got to go away to college and who could actually walk to each other's houses or to a store.)

Virtually riding along the back road (we thought it was a big deal to ride our bikes back there even though we could still see our house), I wondered what happened to everyone. Over the years, after my parents had also moved, there were some news briefs—Mrs. Hines died, there was a horrible boating accident and two other neighbors died by drowning, Uncle Bob refused to move after Aunt Tetia and my cousin Susie died, a few new houses were built—but looking at the old houses I suddenly wanted to know what had become of everyone.

A few years ago, in a crazy nostalgic phase, I thought about writing a book called The Girls From Big Bend. I was going to contact all the girls I knew and write a nonfiction book about them and Big Bend and what happens to small town girls. Remembering this bright idea made me wander "uptown," which was really nothing more than a doctor's office, a store that opened and closed about fifty times when I was growing up, a bank, a couple of taverns, a gas station, and the one place that directed my life—the public library.

The library had moved but not much else had changed, and wandering through the town kickstarted so many other memories I felt as if I had been transported back in time. Our world back then—without cell phones, and computers, and two working parents, and exotic trips, and fancy stores, and excess money—was an amazing gift that kept us grounded and filled with what is really most important in life... even if we sometimes didn't think so.

It's amazing how many memories can rise up through the years of debris with a seemingly simple glimpse of the place where my life was launched. There was a part of me, quite a large part, that always felt as if there was more to life than Big Bend and that I had to go find it, see for myself, and then come back, which of course I did only for visits. I remember sitting alone a lot, reading under the tree in the backyard that I couldn't quite see on my computer today, and dreaming like the small town girl I was about places that were much bigger than Large Lump.

The day I really left, and headed toward Montana in my 4-wheel-drive Toyota with Radishes painted on the side, my parents woke at 4 a.m. to say goodbye. The night before, my father had come into the little room they had turned into a den when we all started getting the hell out of there. He'd sat on the bed next to me, put his rough hands on my face, and told me he was proud of me and that he couldn't believe I had graduated from college because he had always wanted to go. On my virtual tour I put my finger where that room must surely still be standing and I wished I could put my arms around my daddy one more time.

I left all those years ago, ready for life, or so I thought, and had a final glimpse of my parents standing by the same garage door my grandpa drove through waving and clutching at each other, their bathrobes blowing in the wind like the wings of a wild bird caught in a freak storm. I'm a big sap so I'm sure I cried, but all I remember is turning the corner by The Blue Heron Restaurant, which is still there, and thinking, "I've waited for this day my whole life." And what a life it's been and continues to be.

I often tell people that you can never go back home if you don't leave. What I now need to tell them is that if you grew up in a town like I did—with loving parents, across the street from a corn field, thirty minutes from a place that is called a city, and surrounded by the magic of small town life—then home is right there in the center of your lovely heart and you can take it with you wherever you go.

I really have no desire to go physically back to Big Bend and wander the streets and recapture all my memories. I'm all about making new ones and experiencing everything possible before my spin here is over. There's Google Earth, of course, and sadly I know that I will be making the same drive past the house with my mother on my brother's lap some day on the way back to the Veteran's Cemetery.

In the meantime I'm thinking about things like the time my dad started the telephone pole in the backyard on fire and had to call his own volunteer fire department, the afternoon Jeff ripped his face open sled riding down Romey's hill, and the one absolutely beautiful time I made my brothers Jeff and Randy and my cousins, Susie and Mike, pause in the field because the way the sun was filtering through the clouds I thought we were being touched by grace.

And we were. We really, really were.

contingency procedures are in effect

ROY KESEY

I did not think I would need Google to write this essay. I had just been home, after all. I had been all manner of home, in fact. The house in Potter Valley where my parents have lived for the past twenty years. The house in Ukiah where I grew up, which is home to most of my pre-college memories. The house in Lakeport where my grandmother lived until very recently, and another house a few miles into the hills where my great-uncle still lives. I went to each of these places in part to observe, to document, to remember. By coincidence, the trip and the invitation to write this essay occurred less than two weeks apart.

I was wrong, in the end. I still needed satellital help. I still needed to look down from above, as if playing... playing what?

Another form of that question: What was I trying to accomplish, looking down at these homes like that? And another: who does that? Who looks down at the world from such heights?

Birds, of course—although the physiology of most species

seems better suited to keeping watch out above and to the sides, and for good reason. There is nothing that can attack a flying bird from below except a hunter with a shotgun, and relatively few species are subject to that sort of attention. People in airplanes and hang-gliders and parachutes and the like, though these experiences don't seem conducive to close study of the overflown.

Spies, scientists, weatherpersons—all those with access to satellite footage. Which, thanks to technology, is now everyone with an Internet connection. Machines that do our looking for us: this is an obsession of mine, one of many.

And who else?

Gods and angels, certainly—the all-knowing/all-powerful/ever-present, and thus seemingly unnecessary army of messengers and guides, provisioners and protectors, sycophants and rescuers, liberators and influencers, encouragers and administrators and soul-bearers at the moment of death. They also work as executioners—perhaps I should have mentioned that first. Herod Agrippa; the Assyrian army; the Egyptians' firstborn children. Others I don't remember. There is so much I don't remember.

("Google, what are the jobs of the angels?")

And astronauts! I almost forgot them. ("Google, how many have there been?") Five hundred and thirty-six thus far, though three only managed sub-orbital flight. (Five hundred and thirty-six. I have not thought about it much, but this is a larger number than I would have guessed.) And does the total include those who achieved lift-off but died before reaching orbit? There have been eighteen astronauts killed in flight thus far. Eighteen—again a larger number than I would have guessed. Eighteen, though there have only been four incidents.

I am rarely asked to guess things by anyone except children, and drunks in bars.

Birds, parachutists, spies and scientists, gods and angels, astronauts. And children, of course. One must never forget the children. It is said that they are our future, though of course this is false. Our future is death. Theirs too.

In general, children look down from things they have climbed. "Trees are the most commonly climbed entity" is a reasonable-sounding fact I just made up. (Google? No?) But the children who climb onto roofs are the ones who interest me here. Not the ones climbing to show off and not those playing games with other children and not those climbing out of sheer delirious energy and not those looking for somewhere quiet to rub one out or sneak a smoke and not those chased by dogs or bullies or step-parents, but those who climb secretly, pursued only by their consciences if at all: those interested in seeing, in knowing, without being seen or known.

Google Earth opens with a circle meant to intimate a hemi-sphere; on my computer, the circle is centered roughly on the Marion Reservoir in east-central Kansas (and I too must zoom well in to learn this). To the upper right, all of Greenland is visible, and Iceland as well, though the latter is skewed by an approximation of curvature. To the upper left all of Alaska can be seen, and part of easternmost Siberia. To the bottom right one can see the full outline of Peru; northern Brazil and a small bit of Argentina can also be made out. To the bottom left there is only water, but it too is mapped in a sense, different blues showing different depths, striations delineating subaquatic ridges and trenches and plains.

Plugging in the relevant street address causes my circle to rotate eastward, and the Rocky Mountains rush toward me the way they would if I were in free-fall and about to bounce. (Bounce: this is a word skydivers use for what happens to those whose parachutes fail to open. Party in the Crater: this is something else they do, gathering at the spot where a colleague bounced, honoring the dead with drink.) As the ground nears and focus tightens, the center-point shifts to California, to northern California, to Mendocino County, to Ukiah itself (and even at this speed I sense that the town is much thinner east-to-west than it ever seemed to me on the ground, though I must have had a sense of this narrowness fairly early on—I was still in junior high when I realized that I needed to get out).

My simulated descent is halted sharply enough to turn my stomach. I am now looking down on the neighborhood in which I grew up; I am hovering at an altitude of 1.25 kilometers and seeing the streets and houses as they looked on 8 August 2013, or so the lower corners of the screen tell me. Where was I that day? Most likely sitting in my current home in Maryland. But it is hard to know for sure, especially without knowing at exactly what time the satellite overflew Ukiah.

The railroad tracks form the frame's right border. Vinewood Park (Frisbee, church softball practice, a fistfight with Nicky Johnson) is centered at the top. The town cemetery holds the top left, and Pomalita Middle School (a place I knew only as somewhere with outdoor tennis and basketball courts that were in terrible shape but often unoccupied) slumps to the lower left.

(Google, when I type "Are ang"—the first seven characters of my query "Are angels immortal?"—into your search bar, the second-most common such search is "Are angels aliens?" And if I stop one character sooner, the second-most common query is "Are animals gay?" What is it about us that leads us to ask you these things? And what is it with second-most-commons?)

I tighten the focus further. As seen from an altitude of seven hundred meters, most of the neighborhood has fallen away, and I am looking down on the oddly-shaped block that I circled thousands of times: on my bike, jogging, walking very late at night. There are more swimming pools now than there were then, I feel certain of this, though I have no way to be sure.

At four hundred meters, the view is limited to the northern section of that block, perhaps thirty houses in all, plus the power station in the upper right corner—one fence I never climbed. At three hundred meters, a clear view of the roof and backyard of the house in which I was raised. At two hundred twenty, that roof fills the screen, but it has also become badly blurred. It does not look as if any children were up there when the satellite passed overhead. A shame.

My parents never knew how often I climbed onto that roof, and will never know, unless they happen to read this essay. (Or else they always knew, and didn't care; or knew, and cared, but decided to let me do it anyway. I do not plan to ask.) The first time—the first several times, in fact—must have been in the company of my father. He'd needed my help with shingling, or cleaning out the gutters, or I'd fouled off a whiffle ball. But once I knew that it was possible, once I was no longer afraid, it became the place I went, and went, and went.

Back to 8 August 2013. Cycling up and down through different altitudes holds my interest for a time, but feels nothing like what a bird would see. There is nothing on these roofs of interest to spies or scientists, nothing to worry gods or angels. Which leaves children. And astronauts.

Incident #1: 24 April 1967. The first-ever death during spaceflight. Vladimir Komarov, alone on Soyuz 1. He re-enters the atmosphere, and the parachute on his capsule fails to open. An article on the front page of that day's *Owosso Argus-Press* says that he fell for more than four miles—something like two minutes of free-fall. (The article to the left is about a series of tornadoes that killed fifty-two people in Chicago, ripped the roof off of a full church near Memphis, dropped baseball-sized hail in Chattanooga. The article below is about the first U.S. airstrikes on MiG airfields in North Vietnam, and a joint offensive by twenty thousand American and South Vietnamese troops in War Zone C.) The crash site is one hundred seventy miles east-southeast of Orenburg; there is now a small park beside the road, and in that park is a column with a bust of Komarov on top. He is also memorialized, like all other cosmonauts killed in service, at the Kremlin Wall Necropolis in Moscow.

Soyuz: the Russian word for Union.

The sandpapery rasp of the thin asphalt shingles. The sloped roof warm against my back as the sun set. The cold cold moon.

Google, explain to me the purpose of sorrow.

Incident #2: 30 June 1971. Three cosmonauts—Georgi Dobrovolski, Viktor Patsayev, Vladislav Volkov—have been docked at the Salyut ("Salute") space station for three weeks. As the descent module undocks from the service module, explosive bolts meant to fire sequentially in fact fire simultaneously, jolting open a breathing ventilation valve. At the landing site deep in Kazakhstan, the recovery team found no noteworthy damage to the outside of the crew capsule, but inside all three men were motionless, their faces marked with bruise-like patches of dark blue, streams of blood leading from their noses and ears. Dobrovolski's body was still warm, and the recovery team gave him CPR, but like the other two he had died of asphyxiation within a minute of depressurization.

There is no clear boundary determining where earth's atmosphere ends and space starts. The Kármán line at one hundred kilometers above sea level is what is generally used to define the beginning of space for the purposes of international treaties and aerospace records. By this definition, Dobrovolski, Patsayev and Volkov are the only humans ever to die in space.

As I mentioned, I went home not long ago. I was there for the five days between Christmas and New Years. It is a relatively uncommon experience, me going home; this time I went because my grandmother was near death and I wanted to see and speak with her again before losing her. As I also mentioned, while in Lake County I paid a visit to my great-uncle—likewise a central figure from my childhood. He is very old and told me that he sees little reason to continue living, but he is not the sort of person to end his life intentionally.

During those same five days, my niece attempted suicide and a close friend told me he has cancer and I went to sit quietly in the cemetery beside two graves—one that of a high school friend, the other a high school acquaintance.

To refer to the whole visit as a Death Tour would be unseemly but precise.

Unseemly but precise: right in my wheelhouse.

The other two incidents were the Space Shuttle disasters.

One upon lift-off, one upon re-entry. Seven Americans aboard the Challenger; six Americans and one Israeli aboard the Columbia. Nowadays some people confuse the two events, I have found. That would be impossible for me.

I was living in Peru when the Columbia disintegrated on 1 February 2003. I do not remember the disaster in much detail. In fact I remember little except feeling sick to my stomach at what seemed an abhorrent repetition.

At 11:40 a.m. on 28 January 1986, I was sitting in Dennis Shannon's Honors English class. The door opened, and Mike Vinding stood before us. We all stared at him and he was smiling, a trembly smile that was not his at all. He could not help it—he knew something we didn't, and it sickened and thrilled him to be the one bearing the news. That period he was taking a class called Message Service, or something, I don't remember exactly—for the most part you did nothing, and occasionally someone asked you to walk a message to a student or teacher somewhere on campus, and so you did, a sort of messenger angel, but for the administration. The message he'd been asked to bring that day had nothing to do with the Space Shuttle—it was the usual, someone's parents had sent word to their kid about something—but that's not what came out first. Mike Vinding, our smirking trembly angel, announced too loudly that the Challenger had blown up.

The words were the wrong size for any of the slots in our brains.

The class next door was Current Events or something like it. The wall between us and them could be accordioned back toward the center of the building. (It is possible that I have a memory of sudden exclamations of dismay coming from the other side of the wall moments earlier, which means the students there had watched the launch live, but perhaps I have fused two memories—perhaps the sounds were instead those of the spectators at Cape Canaveral whom we would later see on the news, spectators we watched watching.) We joined the other students, filtered in among them. They already had the television tuned to CNN, and turned to us as we entered, looked at us with little content in their expressions except, A big and awful thing has happened, and What does it mean?

Google, what does it mean?

No? All right. But at least you can show it to me again. Google, I deserve no better. Show it to me again.

CNN—still a novelty at this point. I flip back and forth along the YouTube time bar, finally pick a starting point: T minus thirteen minutes. It is a sports segment. An anchor with comically '80s clothes and hair and mustache is reporting on a press conference in which Mike Ditka says little at length about how hard it will be for the Bears to repeat as Super Bowl champions. Then the anchor reports that three members of the University of Minnesota basketball team have been charged with sexual assault following an incident in Wisconsin. There is a teaser for the long-delayed Space Shuttle launch. A teaser for a segment on a couple who exchanged wedding vows under-water. An ad for the all new Mercury Sable, and my stomach begins to tighten. An ad for CNN itself—there is an argument to be made that this is what the network does best. William Hartley on what he calls a "good old-fashioned rally" in the stock market: the DOW has rocketed up to 1547.01. My breathing is growing shallow. A disagreement between King Hussein and Yasser Arafat regarding the necessary preconditions for the establishment of a Palestinian state on the West Bank and in Gaza. Bishop Desmond Tutu calls for worldwide economic sanctions against the South African government unless it changes its Apartheid policies, and no one knows anything about what is to come.

At T minus three minutes, the anchors welcome Tom Mintier, a CNN correspondent who acknowledges that this is not an ideal moment to be launching the Space Shuttle given the improbable cold, but says that the ice has been cleared off the vessel, and that "Challenger should be going away very soon." We then have a live take of the shuttle on the launch pad at Kennedy Space Center, and hear the voice of Hugh Harris from Launch Control as the sequence proceeds.

T minus two minutes and forty-four seconds. Mintier offers information on the mission—a $100 million satellite will be released, as well as another set to study Halley's Comet—and on its true point of interest, the civilian astronaut, high school teacher Christa McAuliffe, the first private citizen to fly into space. It was never clear to me why she was there—not why she was chosen from among eleven thousand applicants, but why a civilian was needed at all. Perhaps it was only as a symbol. A door. The dream: that soon, anyone at all could have a chance to look down from those heights.

T minus one minute and forty-five seconds. "The computers have taken control now," says Mintier. Then Harris' voice again, a faint hiss of static enfolding it: "The liquid hydrogen tank now at flight pressure and all three engines ready to go."

T minus forty seconds. "The solid rocket booster flight instrumentation recorders have gone into the record mode." T minus ten seconds. A first puff of smoke as the hydrogen igniters are lit to burn off residual gas. T minus five seconds, and the main engines fire.

Lift-off, and for the next seventy-two seconds all seems perfect. The shuttle rises slowly, rolls smoothly, borne on its pillar of fire. A new voice now, with a slight Southern accent: NASA public affairs officer Steve Nesbitt. He narrates the early moments of the flight, tells us that all is as it should be. A strange moment beginning at T plus fifty seconds as the shuttle goes out of focus several times, but each time the lens is adjusted and now we see clearly again, or as clearly as possible given the distance and speed and angle. Mintier's voice takes over once again to say, "So the twenty-fifth Space Shuttle mission is now on the way, after more delays than NASA cares to count. This morning it looked as though they were not going to be able to get off... "

That ellipsis is Mintier's, not mine. His rising voice is left hanging, interrupted by the raging world. Just as the camera feed shifts to show us the shuttle in profile, there is a flare of flame from the near side, a larger flame from the far side, and in the next instant all is taken in soundless fire.

There is a bizarre disjunct as Nesbitt informs us of the velocity, altitude, and downrange distance of a vessel that is no longer intact. For a moment the screen is filled with smoke. When the camera pulls back, it shows two white plumes: the solid rocket boosters shooting off each to its side, then correcting and continuing on in rough parallel against that stark blue sky. The camera pulls back further, the image now that of something unrelated to flight in any sense, something randomly chosen and minimally evolved, some harmless simple strange creature—say, an albino snail sliding across a skylight. Then the angle changes, and the image is that of horns, the horns of some evil white billowing god.

There is faint bedlam—the reactions of engineers at Flight Control, or perhaps of studio staff. The camera tracks the contrails of falling debris—it begins with a single silent take more than twenty seconds long. Nesbitt's voice breaks as he tells us that contingency procedures are in effect. And that is enough. I remember what comes in the next minutes, hours, days: abhorrent repetition interspersed with inanity, and then explanations, excuses, accusations. Because we are human. Because we are afraid.

Google, please list all unknowables.

The high school I attended is right across the street from the cemetery. I haven't been on the school grounds more than a handful of times since I graduated in 1986, but I visit the cemetery every time I go home, or very nearly so. It is a beautiful space: the southeast and northwest corners are mostly grass, and the rest is shaded by trees, some of them immense cedars and redwoods. In the fall and winter, the gravel paths are lined with fallen leaves. There are squirrels and chipmunks. Robins, jays, starlings. Moss on the older headstones. It is as pleasant a place to end up as any other, I think.

One of the things I like about the cemetery is how little it changes, but this last time it held a surprise: a herd of deer, fifteen or so, lying in the shade behind the chapel. One by one they stood and walked off as I neared. Two of them were bucks, the biggest one a magnificent animal, antlers twenty inches high and nearly that wide, a three-by-four with a single eye guard an inch long. He'd be one of the biggest bucks I'd ever killed if I'd killed him.

The graves I come to visit are never quite where I remember them, though I've been here a dozen times at least. There is a massive valley oak, the biggest tree in the northwest corner. One grave is just southwest of it, the other a little farther southeast. I cleared off the leaves, wiped away a little mud. Sat down. Watched the day. To the north is a vineyard, just naked brown vines this time of year. To the south is the Mendocino County Jail. To the west is the high school. Beyond the school are the hills. Beyond the hills, that day, a blurred sliver of moon, or so I choose to remember it.

And do you remember the parachute? T plus eight minutes and forty-six seconds, Google says. White against the sky, full and slow. The camera tracked it as it fell, and it was impossible for us to make out what it carried, and so for a moment we were able to hope. Someone in the newsroom clapped briefly. Nesbitt broke in, said something about paramedics. In fact it was only a drogue parachute carrying the nose cap of one of the boosters. Debris was still raining down, and no one would enter the crash site for another forty minutes.

From the roof I watched neighbors and imagined they were escapees from the jail. I watched dogs and imagined they were bears. I watched squirrels, and every so often a deer, and always the birds—robin, jay, starling.

I am indifferent, perhaps oddly so, to the notion of being a bird. But I am thinking now that I would like to be a spy, or an astronaut, or a god, or a child. It is too late for any of those things, however. My grandmother and I had several chances to talk, each brief but full. She died seven weeks after I left. It is too late for most things but not all.

GRANT JARRETT

credit: Yoshi

Originally from northeastern Pennsylvania, Grant Jarrett currently lives in Manhattan, where he works as a writer, ghostwriter, editor, musician, and occasional songwriter. His publishing credits include magazine articles, short stories, and *More Towels*, his coming-of-age memoir about life on the road. His debut novel, *Ways of Leaving*, won the Best New Fiction category of the 2014 International Book Award. In their glowing review of *Ways of Leaving*, *Kirkus Reviews* said, "Ruthlessly brilliant writing brings grace to a story smoldering in pain."

Find out more at www.grantjarrett.com

J E F F E R Y   R E N A R D   A L L E N

credit: Mark Hillringhouse

Jeffery Renard Allen is Professor of Creative Writing at the University of Virginia. Allen is the author of five books, most recently the novel *Song of the Shank* (Graywolf Press, 2014), which is loosely based on the life of Blind Tom, a nineteenth-century African-American piano virtuoso and composer who was the first African-American to perform at the White House. The novel was a finalist for the IMPAC Award, and featured as the front-page review of both *The New York Times Book Review* and *San Francisco Chronicle*. It won the Firecracker Award and was also a finalist for the PEN/Faulkner Award. Allen's novel *Rails Under My Back* won the *Chicago Tribune*'s Heartland Prize for Fiction, and his short story collection *Holding Pattern* won the Ernest J. Gaines Award for Literary Excellence. Allen has received other accolades for his work, including a Whiting Writers' Award, a grant in Innovative Literature from Creative Capital, and most recently a Guggenheim Fellowship. His website is www.jefferyrenardallen.com.

ALICE EVE COHEN

Alice Eve Cohen is a playwright, solo theatre artist, and award-winning author of two memoirs, *The Year My Mother Came Back* and *What I Thought I Knew*, which was winner of the *Elle* Magazine Literary Grand Prix for Nonfiction, *O: the Oprah Magazine*'s 25 Best Books of Summer, and *Salon*'s Best Books of the Year. Cohen has written for Nickelodeon & CTW and has toured her solo plays internationally. She received a B.A. from Princeton and an M.F.A. from The New School. She teaches playwriting and creative writing at The New School.

PAMELA ERENS

credit: Kathryn Huang

Pamela Erens is the author of the novels *Eleven Hours*, *The Virgins*, and *The Understory*, all from Tin House Books. She has been a finalist for the *Los Angeles Times* Book Prize for First Fiction, the William Saroyan International Prize for Writing, and the John Gardner Fiction Book Award. *The Virgins* was named a *New York Times* and *Chicago Tribune* Editors' Choice and a Best Book of 2013 by *The New Yorker*, *The New Republic*, *Salon*, and *Library Journal*. Erens's essays and criticism have appeared in *Virginia Quarterly Review*, *The Los Angeles Review of Books*, *The New York Times*, *The Millions*, *Vogue*, and *Elle*. She considers herself essentially a New Yorker.

RU FREEMAN

credit: Brenda Carpenter

Ru Freeman is a Sri Lankan-born speaker, activist, and writer whose work has appeared internationally. She is the author of the novels *A Disobedient Girl* (Atria/Simon & Schuster, 2009) and *On Sal Mal Lane* (Graywolf, 2013), both of which have been translated into multiple languages, and editor of a forthcoming anthology of American writers writing about Palestine, *Extraordinary Rendition* (OR Books). She is the 2014 winner of the Janet Heidinger Kafka Prize for Fiction by an American Woman. She blogs for the Huffington Post on literature and politics.

ROY KESEY

credit: Ana Lucía Nieto

Roy Kesey's latest books are the short story collection *Any Deadly Thing* (Dzanc Books, 2013) and the novel *Pacazo* (Dzanc Books, 2011/Jonathan Cape, 2012). He is the winner of an NEA grant for fiction and a PEN/Heim grant for translation. His short stories, essays, translations and poems have appeared in about a hundred magazines and anthologies, including *Best American Short Stories* and *New Sudden Fiction*.

credit: Marion Ettlinger

Porochista Khakpour is a novelist, essayist, journalist, and professor. She is the author of the forthcoming memoir *Sick* (Harper-
Perennial, 2017) and the novels *The Last Illusion* (Bloomsbury,
2014)—a 2014 "Best Book of the Year" according to NPR, *Kirkus*,
Buzzfeed, Popmatters, Electric Literature, and more—and *Sons
and Other Flammable Objects* (Grove, 2007), which was the
2007 California Book Award winner in "First Fiction," one of the
Chicago Tribune's "Fall's Best," and a *New York Times* "Editor's
Choice." She has had fellowships from the NEA, Yaddo, Ucross,
the Sewanee Writers' Conference, Northwestern University, the
University of Leipzig, and many others. Her writing has appeared
or is forthcoming in *Harper's*, *The New York Times*, *The Los Angeles
Times*, *The Wall Street Journal*, *Al Jazeera America*, *Bookforum*, *Slate*,
Salon, *Spin*, *The Daily Beast*, *Elle*, and many other publications
around the world. She is currently contributing editor at The
Offing, a channel of *The Los Angeles Review of Books*, and Writer
in Residence at Bard College. Born in Tehran and raised in Los
Angeles, she lives in New York City.

TIM JOHNSTON

credit: Dave Boerger

Tim Johnston is the author of the novel *Descent* (2015, Algonquin), the story collection *Irish Girl* (2009, UNT Press), and the young adult novel *Never So Green* (2002, Farrar, Straus & Giroux). A *New York Times, USA Today*, and *Indie National* bestseller, *Descent* is in its fifth printing and has been optioned for film. The stories in *Irish Girl* have won an O. Henry Prize, the *New Letters* Award for Writers, and the Gival Press Short Story Award, while the collection itself won the 2009 Katherine Anne Porter Prize in Short Fiction. Tim holds degrees from the University of Iowa and the University of Massachusetts, Amherst. He is the 2015 Iowa Author, and currently teaches in the Creative Writing Program at the University of Memphis.

PAUL MCVEIGH

Paul McVeigh was born in Belfast where he began his writing career in theatre. He moved to London where he wrote comedy shows, some of which appeared in London's West End. His short fiction has been published in journals and anthologies, been commissioned by *BBC Radio 4*, and read on *BBC Radio 5*. His debut novel *The Good Son* was published in April 2015 and has been called 'a work of genius' by Pulitzer Prize-winner Robert Olen Butler and 'stunningly intelligent' by Laura van den Berg, who calls McVeigh 'a wildly important new talent.' Paul is Director of the London Short Story Festival and Associate Director at Word Factory, the UK's leading short story salon.

ELLEN MEISTER

credit: dearellen

Ellen Meister is the author of five novels, including *Dorothy Parker Drank Here* (Putnam, 2015), *Farewell, Dorothy Parker* (Putnam, 2013), *The Other Life* (Putnam, 2011), and *The Smart One* (HarperCollins, 2008). Her honors include being selected for the prestigious Indie Next List, foreign language translations of her work, appearances on NPR, and receiving a TV series option from HBO. Her nonfiction has appeared in *Publishers Weekly, The New York Times, The Wall Street Journal* blog, *Huffington Post, Daily Beast, Long Island Woman, Writer's Digest,* and more. Ellen mentors emerging authors, and does public speaking about her books and about Dorothy Parker and the Algonquin Round Table. For more information visit her website at:

www.ellenmeister.com.

JULIE METZ

credit: Sigrid Estrada

Julie Metz is the author of *Perfection*, a *New York Times* bestseller and a Barnes & Noble Discover New Writers Selection. In addition to her work as a graphic designer for Sparkpoint, she has written on a variety of women's issues for publications such as *The New York Times*, *Salon*, *Dame*, *Redbook*, *Huffington Post*, *Glamour*, *Coastal Living*, and mrbellersneighborhood.com. A born and raised New Yorker, she currently lives and works in the Hudson River Valley. You can find out more at:

www.juliemetz.com

JEN MICHALSKI

credit: Phuong Huynh

Jen Michalski is the author of the novels *The Tide King* (Black Lawrence Press, 2013) and *The Summer She Was Under Water* (QFP, 2016), two collections of fiction, and a couplet of novellas, *Could You Be With Her Now* (Dzanc Books, 2013). She also edited the collection *City Sages: Baltimore* (CityLit Press, 2010). She hosts the fiction series Starts Here! in Baltimore, edits the journal *jmww*, and tweets at @MichalskiJen.

LAURA MILLER

Laura Miller is a journalist and critic living in New York. She is a co-founder of Salon.com, where she is currently a staff writer. Her work has appeared in *The New Yorker, Harper's, The Guardian,* and *The New York Times Book Review,* where she wrote the "Last Word" column for two years. She is the author of *The Magician's Book: A Skeptic's Adventures in Narnia* (Little, Brown, 2008) and editor of *The Salon.com Reader's Guide to Contemporary Authors* (Penguin, 2000).

JUSTINE MUSK

Justine Musk has been published in *Time, Newsweek, Entrepreneur, Inc., Marie Claire,* and others. She is the author of three traditionally published dark fantasy novels and blogs about falling into your bigger story at justinemusk.com. She lives in Los Angeles with her sons and a young Labradoodle who is eating his way through her shoe collection.

credit: Dana Kroos

Antonya Nelson is the author of four novels, including *Bound* (Bloomsbury, 2010), and seven short story collections, including *Funny Once* (Bloomsbury, 2014). Her work has appeared in *The New Yorker*, *Esquire*, *Harper's*, *Redbook*, and many other magazines, as well as in anthologies such as *Prize Stories: the O. Henry Awards* and *Best American Short Stories*. She is the recipient of a USA Artists Award in 2009, the 2003 Rea Award for Short Fiction, as well as NEA and Guggenheim Fellowships. She teaches in the Warren Wilson M.F.A. Program, as well as in the University of Houston's Creative Writing Program. She lives in Telluride, Colorado, Las Cruces, New Mexico, and Houston, Texas.

Kris Radish is the bestselling author of ten novels and three works of non-fiction. Her empowering books focus on the very *real* issues women face in their lives, and she celebrates the important and amazing power of female friendship via her novels and in her yearly retreats held for women from across the globe. She is a former working journalist, editor, university lecturer, bureau chief, nationally syndicated columnist, magazine writer, worm picker, professional Girl Scout and lifeguard—to name but a few of her past experiences. Radish is also co-owner of the Wine Madonna wine lounge in downtown St. Petersburg, Florida and Radish & Company Boutique, where she hosts book groups and special events and does a bit of wine drinking herself. Radish is also working on her eleventh novel and a second book of autobiographical essays.

MEG TUITE

Meg Tuite is the author of two short story collections, *Bound By Blue* (Sententia Books, 2013) and *Domestic Apparition* (San Francisco Bay Press, 2011), three chapbooks, and a forthcoming prose/poetry chapbook co-written with David Tomaloff. She won the Twin Antlers Collaborative Poetry Award from Artistically Declined Press for her poetry collection, *Bare Bulbs Swinging* (2014), co-written with Heather Fowler and Michelle Reale. She teaches at Santa Fe Community College, is fiction editor for *The Santa Fe Literary Review*, and writes a featured column for Connotation Press and a column at *jmww*. She lives in Santa Fe with her husband and a menagerie of pets. Her blog: http://megtuite.com.

credit: CeCe Ziolkowski

Lee Upton's collection of short stories, *The Tao of Humiliation*, was selected as one of the "best books of 2014" by *Kirkus Reviews*, received the BOA Short Fiction Award, was a finalist for the Paterson Prize, and received starred reviews from both *Kirkus* and *Library Journal*. Her sixth collection of poetry, *Bottle the Bottles the Bottles the Bottles*, a recipient of the Open Book Award, appeared in May 2015 from the Cleveland State University Poetry Center. She is the author of fourteen books, including the novella *The Guide to the Flying Island*, the essay collection *Swallowing the Sea: On Writing & Ambition, Boredom, Purity & Secrecy*, and four books of literary criticism. She is the Francis A. March Professor of English and Writer-in-Residence at Lafayette College.

PATRICIA JABBEH WESLEY

Patricia Jabbeh Wesley is a survivor of the Liberian civil war, immigrating to the United States in 1991. She is the author of four books of poetry: *Where the Road Turns*, *The River is Rising*, *Becoming Ebony* and *Before the Palm Could Bloom: Poems of Africa*. Her fifth book of poetry is forthcoming. She is also the author of one children's book, *In Monrovia, the River Visits the Sea*, published in 2013. She has won several awards and grants including the 2011 President Barack Obama Award for her poetry from Blair County NAACP, the 2010 Liberian Award for her poetry, a Penn State University AESEDA Collaborative Grant for her research on Liberian women's trauma stories, a 2002 Crab Orchard Award for her second book of poems, *Becoming Ebony*, and several artist grants from the Kalamazoo Foundation, among others. Patricia has been a featured poet and speaker both in the United States and internationally, and her poetry has been critically acclaimed by many reviewers and scholarly publications worldwide. She has also published dozens of individual poems and memoir articles in many American and international journals and anthologies, including *The New Orleans Review*, *Crab Orchard Review*, *English Academy Review of South Africa*, *The Prometeo Magazine* and in the Bedford/St. Martin's textbook *Approaching Literature: Writing, Reading, Thinking* (2nd & 3rd editions), among others. Most recently, her memoir article, "Erecting Stones," was published in *Coal Hill Review*. She teaches Creative Writing and Literature at Penn State University, USA.

ACKNOWLEDGMENTS

by Grant Jarrett

Special thanks to Joanna and Yoshi for believing in me (or at least pretending to), to Crystal and the entire staff at Spark Press for becoming infected with my enthusiasm (or at least mimicking the symptoms), to my cycling buddies Jenn and Sean for listening to me whine about how difficult it is to put an anthology together (or falling back to avoid listening and to boost my fragile athlete's ego), and to all the talented authors who joined me in this endeavor (several of whom still occasionally respond to my emails).

Finally, with the understanding that, although their recollections of our shared past certainly wouldn't mirror my own, they might occasionally intersect, I'd like to thank my four brothers, my mother, and my father for helping to create the atmosphere that to some degree made us all the people we ultimately became—flawed and floundering, but mostly trying our best.

SELECTED TITLES FROM SPARKPRESS

SparkPress is an independent boutique publisher
delivering high-quality, entertaining, and engaging
content that enhances readers' lives.
Visit us at www.gosparkpress.com

Ways of Leaving, by Grant Jarrett. $15, 978-1-94071-641-1. A
standout novel about going home, where old girlfriends,
awkward funerals, deeply buried parental secrets and naked
drunken, nocturnal escapades irritate a man like scabs of
squandered youth and misspent adulthood.

Gravel on the Side of the Road, by Kris Radish. $15,
978-1-94071-643-5. A woman who nearly drowns in a desert
canyon, flies into the war in Bosnia, dances with the FBI, tells
Geraldo he shouldn't put guests in hotel rooms with rats, and
spends time with murderers has more than a few stories to tell.

The House of Bradbury, by Nicole Meier. $17, 978-1-940716-38-1.
After Mia Gladwell's debut novel bombs and her fiancé jumps
ship, she purchases the estate of iconic author Ray Bradbury,
hoping it will inspire her best work yet. But between her disap-
proving sister, mysterious sketches that show up on her door,
and taking in a pill-popping starlet as a tenant—a favor to her
needy ex—life in the Bradbury house is not what she imagined.